easy baking

easy baking

simple recipes for cakes, cookies, pies, and breads

Linda Collister

RYLAND
PETERS
& SMALL

LONDON NEW YORK

Designer Luana Gobbo

Commissioning Editor
Elsa Petersen-Schepelern

Editor Sharon Ashman

Production Paul Harding

Art Director Gabriella Le Grazie

Publishing Director Alison Starling

For Alan

First published as *Linda Collister's Book of Baking* in the United States in 2004

This edition published in 2008
by Ryland Peters & Small, Inc.
519 Broadway, 5th Floor
New York, NY 10012
www.rylandpeters.com

10 9 8 7 6 5 4 3 2 1

ISBN: 978 1 84597 745 0

The original hardcover edition is cataloged as follows:
Library of Congress
Cataloging-in-Publication Data

Collister, Linda.
 Linda Collister's book of baking : delicious recipes for cakes, cookies, pies, and breads.
 p. cm.
 Recipes previously published 2003 by Ryland Peters & Small as Chocolate temptations, Scrumptious pies and tarts, Irresistible cookies and biscotti, and Flavored breads.
 Includes index.
 ISBN 1-84172-711-3
 1. Baking. 2. Desserts. I. Title: Book of baking. II. Collister, Linda. Chocolate temptations. III. Collister, Linda. Scrumptious pies & tarts. IV. Collister, Linda. Irresistible cookies & biscotti V. Collister, Linda. Flavored breads. VI. Title.
 TX765.C615 2004
 641.8'15–dc22
                                    2004000315

Printed in China

Notes:
All spoon measurements are level unless otherwise specified. One teaspoon is 5 ml, 1 tablespoon is 15 ml.

Before baking, weigh or measure all ingredients exactly, and prepare baking pans or trays. Weighing scales and a set of cup measures are recommended for use with these recipes.

Ovens should be preheated to the specified temperature. I recommend using an oven thermometer and consulting the manufacturer's handbook for special instructions.

Uncooked eggs should not be served to the very young, the very old, people with compromised immune systems, or to pregnant women.

Most of the breads in this book can be frozen for up to 1 month. The exceptions are Bacon and Walnut Fougasses (page 186), Cherry Tomato Focaccia with Basil (page 191), and Rye and Caraway Loaf (page 202), which should not be frozen.

The recipes in this book have previously been published by Ryland Peters & Small, Inc. as *Chocolate Temptations*, *Scrumptious Pies & Tarts*, *Irresistible Cookies & Biscotti*, and *Flavored Breads*.

contents

the joy of baking

Why bother baking at home when the supermarkets are desperate to sell you ready-made breads, cakes, and cookies?

Because nothing beats the real thing, homemade: an honest sponge cake that tastes of real, good butter and fresh eggs; pastry that truly melts in the mouth; bread with flavor, a good texture, and chewy crust; cookies reeking of real vanilla; intense pure chocolate desserts. The fact is that quality ingredients result in high-quality flavor.

For me, baking combines so many pleasures: the creative pride of making something, social satisfaction in the sharing of my spoils, and the sensual delight in the eating. My recipes are made for sharing.

Obviously to use this book you need an oven. You cannot bake well without a good, controllable oven. I've used a lot of ovens over the years, from bottled-gas stoves in remote log cabins, to ultra-modern, top-of-the-range appliances, and from solid fuel cast-iron ranges to wood-fired brick ovens. As a result, I have found that an oven thermometer is an essential piece of equipment. Thermostats are often unreliable and you need to know how your oven behaves, so get an inexpensive thermometer and check your oven. The cooking times given in this book are guidelines; your oven handbook and your experience will teach you which shelf works best for you.

If you do a lot of baking, heavy-duty professional-quality pans and trays are a good investment. They will not buckle or scorch in the oven or rust after washing, and should last a lifetime. Non-stick baking parchment is particularly useful for lining baking trays when making meringues or delicate cookies, and a large wire cooling rack is very convenient for everything from cookies to bread.

The two other pieces of equipment I use most are a large, free-standing electric mixer, which makes cake batter, whisks egg whites, and kneads bread dough; and a food processor. Hard though this is to admit, these days I would not make dough without a food processor—my machine does a far better job than my hands.

Have fun—bake something simple and irresistible.

chocolate
baking

the food of the gods

Eating chocolate is pure joy, cooking with it a delight, even smelling it is bewitching, but buying it shakes my faith in human nature. The best chocolate is wonderful, but much of it is not worth buying and most people buy terrible stuff. Good quality bittersweet chocolate will taste smooth not greasy, bitter not raw, intense not oversweet, with a long finish, not an excessively sweet aftertaste.

But how do you know good quality? Price is not a reliable guide—in fact supermarkets' own brands are usually excellent and are a good bargain when buying in bulk for cooking.

The quality and taste of chocolate is determined by the quantity and quality of the cocoa solids—the dry solids plus the added cocoa butter—used in its production. American bittersweet chocolate or European dark luxury chocolate such as Lindt is best for baking. Bittersweet has around 35 percent cocoa solids, whereas Lindt—which is widely available in good supermarkets and specialty shops—has up to 70 percent. Couverture chocolate produces a glossy surface, and is used by professional bakers.

The raw material for chocolate is the cocoa bean, found in the large yellow-green fruits of the *Theobroma cacao* tree which grows only within 20 degrees north or south of the equator. Each tree yields enough beans to make around 5 lb. of chocolate each year. The best chocolate is made from a blend of beans—each type has its own individual character and color, ranging from pale coffee through to dark mahogany brown.

Store chocolate away from other foods in an airtight container in a cool, dry place, because it can easily be tainted by other flavors. Avoid storing chocolate below 55°F, or in the refrigerator, as beads of moisture will form when you bring it to room temperature.

Don't store in a hot kitchen (85°F or above) or it will develop a white bloom as the cocoa butter comes to the surface. The bloom does not affect its taste however—it can still used for cooking. Chocolate begins melting at 85°F (that's why it melts in the mouth) and burns at 228°F.

To melt chocolate, chop it into evenly-sized pieces so it melts at the same rate. Place in the top of a double boiler or in a shallow, heatproof bowl set over a saucepan of steaming hot, not boiling, water. The water must not touch the base of the bowl, and no drop of water or steam should touch the chocolate or it will seize up. Melt it slowly and gradually since it easily becomes overheated and scorched, and turns into an unusable solid mass. Stir frequently, and remove from the heat as soon as it melts.

CHOCOLATE CAKES

almond chocolate kugelhopf

2⅔ cups white bread flour

½ teaspoon sea salt

0.6 oz. cake compressed yeast*

5 tablespoons sugar

¾ cup plus 1 tablespoon
skim milk, lukewarm

3 eggs, beaten

2½ oz. bittersweet chocolate,
coarsely chopped

7 tablespoons unsalted butter,
softened

½ cup slivered almonds

confectioners' sugar, for dusting

Nut Coating

2 tablespoons unsalted butter,
softened

½ cup slivered almonds

*a Kugelhopf mold or Bundt pan,
9 inches diameter*

Makes 1 large cake

**To use easy-blend dried yeast, mix
1 package with 1 cup of the flour.
Mix in the sugar and milk and let
rise for 30 minutes. Make a well in
the remaining flour, add the salt,
then the yeast liquid and eggs, and
proceed with the recipe.*

To make the nut coating, spread the softened butter thickly inside the Kugelhopf mold, then press the almonds all around. Chill while preparing the dough.

To make the dough, put the flour and salt in a large bowl and mix, then make a well in the center.

Crumble the yeast into a small bowl, add the sugar and lukewarm milk, then cream to a smooth liquid. Pour into the well in the flour, and work in enough flour to make a thick batter.

Cover with a damp cloth, and leave at normal room temperature for 30 minutes. The batter should look bubbly. Add the eggs to the yeast liquid, stir until mixed, then gradually beat in the flour to make a soft and very sticky dough. Beat the dough in the bowl with your hand or with the dough hook in an electric mixer for about 5 minutes or until it becomes firmer, smooth, very elastic, and shiny.

Chop the chocolate and add it, along with the softened butter and almonds to the bowl, and work in until thoroughly mixed. Carefully spoon the soft dough into the prepared mold (it should be half-full).

Cover the mold with a damp cloth and let rise at normal room temperature until the dough has almost doubled in size and has risen to about 1 inch below the rim of the mold—about 1 hour.

Bake in a preheated oven at 400°F for about 45 minutes or until the cake is golden brown and a skewer inserted midway between the outer edge and inner tube comes out clean. Remove from the oven and let cool in the mold for 1 minute, then carefully unmold onto a wire rack and let cool completely. Serve dusted with confectioners' sugar.

Store in an airtight container and eat within 3 days, or freeze for up to 1 month. It can be lightly toasted under a broiler.

VARIATIONS

Marbled Kugelhopf

Replace ⅓ cup of the white bread flour with ½ cup sifted unsweetened cocoa powder and 2 tablespoons sugar. Replace the 2½ oz. bittersweet chocolate with a similar quantity of white chocolate, coarsely chopped. Proceed as in the main recipe.

Golden Raisin Kugelhopf

Replace ⅓ cup of the white bread flour with ½ cup sifted unsweetened cocoa powder and 2 tablespoons sugar. Replace the 2½ oz. bittersweet chocolate with ⅓ cup golden raisins or raisins. Proceed as in the main recipe.

NOTE: Both variations are delicious toasted, and spread with butter or peanut butter.

This pretty, yeast coffee-time cake is made in a traditional earthenware mold, a tube pan, or non-stick ring mold. Serve it either plain or toasted.

chocolate gingerbread

A great combination of bittersweet chocolate and ginger in syrup.

Chop the chocolate and melt it very gently in the top of a double boiler or in a heatproof bowl set over a saucepan of steaming, not boiling, water. Stir until smooth, remove the bowl from the heat, and let cool. Using an electric mixer or wooden spoon, beat the butter until creamy, then gradually beat in the sugar. Beat until light and fluffy, then beat in the egg yolks, one at a time, beating well after each addition.

Beat in the cooled chocolate, then sift the almonds, flour, and cocoa into the bowl. Add the 3 pieces chopped ginger and syrup, and fold in gently using a large metal spoon.

In a separate bowl, whisk the egg whites until stiff peaks form, then fold into the chocolate mixture in 3 batches.

Spoon the mixture into the prepared pan and smooth the surface. Bake in a preheated oven at 375°F for about 40 minutes or until a skewer inserted into the center of the cake comes out clean. Remove from the oven, let cool in the pan for 5 minutes, then turn out onto a wire rack and let cool completely.

To make the topping, chop the chocolate and melt it with the butter and ginger syrup in the top of a double boiler or in a heatproof bowl set over a saucepan of steaming, not boiling, water. Stir until smooth, then spoon over the top of the cake. When almost set, decorate with finely sliced, diced, or grated preserved ginger.

Store in an airtight container and eat within 1 week—it improves in taste after several days. If undecorated, it can be frozen for up to 1 month.

5½ oz. bittersweet chocolate

1⅓ sticks unsalted butter, at room temperature

¾ cup sugar

3 large eggs, separated

½ cup plus 1 tablespoon ground almonds

¾ cup plus 1½ tablespoons self-rising flour

1 tablespoon unsweetened cocoa powder

3 pieces preserved ginger, chopped

2 tablespoons syrup from jar of preserved ginger

Chocolate Topping

1½ oz. bittersweet chocolate, chopped

1 tablespoon unsalted butter

1 piece of preserved ginger, finely sliced, and 1 tablespoon syrup from the jar, to finish

a loaf pan, 8½ x 4½ x 2½ inches, greased and lined with baking parchment

Makes 1 cake

marbled fudge cake

This cake improves in flavor for several days after baking.

To make the graham cracker crust, melt the butter, add the crushed graham crackers, and mix well. Press the mixture into the bottom of the pan to make a thin, even layer. Chill while preparing the filling.

To make the chocolate mixture, dice the butter and bring to room temperature. Chop the chocolate and melt it gently in the top of a double boiler or in a heatproof bowl set over a saucepan of steaming, not boiling, water. Stir until smooth, remove the bowl from the heat, and stir in the butter.

In a separate bowl, beat the eggs and sugar with a wooden spoon until frothy. Sift the flour, salt, and baking powder into the bowl and stir well. Add the melted chocolate mixture and the vanilla extract. Chop the nuts, add to the bowl, and mix well. Spread the mixture over the graham cracker crust in the pan.

To make the vanilla mixture, bring the butter to room temperature, then beat until creamy using a wooden spoon or electric mixer. Beat in the vanilla extract and cream cheese until the mixture is light and fluffy. Gradually beat in the sugar, then the egg. Add the flour and stir well.

Spoon the mixture on top of the chocolate layer in the pan. Swirl the tip of a knife through both mixtures to give a marbled effect.

Bake in a preheated oven at 350°F for about 25 minutes or until just firm. Remove from the oven and let cool in the pan before unmolding. Serve at room temperature.

Store in an airtight container and eat within 5 days, or freeze for up to 1 month.

½ stick unsalted butter

3 oz. graham crackers, crushed

Chocolate Mixture

3 tablespoons unsalted butter

4 oz. bittersweet chocolate

2 large eggs

¾ cup sugar

½ cup all-purpose flour

a pinch of salt

½ teaspoon baking powder

2–3 drops real vanilla extract

2 oz. walnut or pecan pieces (about ½ cup)

Vanilla Mixture

1½ tablespoons unsalted butter

½ teaspoon real vanilla extract

⅓ cup cream cheese

¼ cup sugar

1 large egg, beaten

1 tablespoon all-purpose flour

a springform pan, 8 inches diameter, greased

Makes 1 cake (16 slices)

espresso cake

1⅔ cups self-rising flour

1 cup minus 1 tablespoon unsweetened cocoa powder

a pinch of salt

1 tablespoon very finely ground espresso coffee

1⅓ cups ground almonds

2 sticks unsalted butter

1 cup superfine or granulated sugar

4 large eggs, beaten

3 tablespoons very hot water

1 tablespoon coffee liqueur or brandy (optional)

Chocolate Frosting

⅔ cup heavy cream

5½ oz. bittersweet chocolate, chopped

1 tablespoon very strong black coffee, coffee liqueur, or brandy

a springform pan, 9 inches diameter, greased and lined with baking parchment

Makes 1 cake

Finely ground espresso coffee rather than liquid coffee may appear to be a rather odd ingredient for this moist cake—but it tastes extraordinarily good!

Sift the flour, cocoa, salt, coffee, and ground almonds together into a bowl.

In a separate bowl, beat the butter until creamy using a wooden spoon or electric mixer. Gradually beat in the sugar, until light and fluffy, then beat in the eggs, 1 tablespoon at a time.

Carefully fold in the dry ingredients, along with the hot water, and coffee liqueur or brandy, if using, with a large metal spoon. Gently spoon the mixture into the prepared springform pan and smooth the surface. Bake in a preheated oven at 350°F for about 40 minutes, or until a skewer inserted into the center of the cake comes out clean. Remove from the oven, carefully loosen the cake, then unclip the pan. Transfer to a wire rack to cool.

To make the chocolate frosting, heat the cream until scalding hot, then remove from the heat and add the chocolate and coffee or alcohol. Leave it until completely melted, then stir gently.

When the frosting is cool and thick enough to spread, use it to cover the top and sides of the cake. Let it set, then store in an airtight container overnight before cutting.

Eat within 1 week, or freeze for up to 1 month.

fudgy nut cake

12 oz. bittersweet chocolate

1½ sticks unsalted butter, diced

½ cup unsweetened cocoa powder, sifted, plus extra for dusting

3½ oz. mixture of nuts (about 1 cup)

5 large eggs

1 teaspoon real vanilla extract

1¼ cups sugar

confectioners' sugar, for dusting

a springform pan, 8 inches diameter, greased and lined with baking parchment

Makes 1 cake

Make this soft, moist, flourless cake with a mixture of nuts, such as macadamias, pecans, walnuts, almonds, or hazelnuts.

Chop the chocolate and put in a heatproof bowl set it over a pan of steaming, not boiling, water, or in the top of a double boiler. Add the diced butter and stir frequently until melted and smooth. Remove the bowl from the heat, stir in the cocoa, and let cool.

Meanwhile, coarsely chop the nuts. Put the eggs, vanilla extract, and sugar in a large heatproof bowl and beat briefly until frothy. Set the bowl over a pan of steaming, not boiling, water—the water should not touch the bottom of the bowl. Using an electric egg beater, beat the mixture until it is very pale and thick—when the beater is lifted it should leave a visible ribbon-like trail.

Remove the bowl from the heat, and beat for a couple of minutes so the mixture cools. Using a large metal spoon, carefully fold in the cooled chocolate mixture, followed by the nuts. When thoroughly combined, spoon into the prepared springform pan and smooth the surface.

Bake in a preheated oven at 350°F for about 35 minutes or until firm to the touch but moist inside (do not overcook or it will be dry and hard to slice).

Remove from the oven and let cool in the pan, then remove from the pan and serve, dusted with confectioners' sugar and cocoa.

Store in an airtight container and eat within 1 week. It does not freeze well.

chocolate pound cake

Rum-soaked golden raisins, butter, sugar, flour, and cocoa—a terrific combination. Don't worry if the fruit sinks during baking.

⅓ **cup golden raisins**

3 tablespoons rum

2 sticks plus 2 tablespoons unsalted butter, at room temperature

1¼ cups superfine or granulated sugar

4 large eggs, at room temperature

½ cup unsweetened cocoa powder

1⅓ cups self-rising flour

a pinch of salt

a loaf pan, 2 lb., lined with a double thickness of greased wax paper

Makes 1 large cake

Put the golden raisins in a bowl, add the rum, cover, and let soak overnight.

Put the soft butter in the bowl of an electric mixer and beat until creamy. Gradually beat in the sugar. After the last addition, beat the mixture until it becomes very pale and light in texture.

Put the eggs in a separate bowl and beat. Add to the butter mixture, 1 tablespoon at a time, beating well after each addition.

Sift the cocoa, flour, and salt twice, then add to the egg mixture. Fold in the dry ingredients very gently using a large metal spoon. When thoroughly combined, fold in the golden raisins, along with any rum left in the bowl.

Spoon the mixture into the prepared pan and smooth the surface. Bake in a preheated oven at 400°F for 40 to 50 minutes or until a toothpick or skewer inserted into the center of the cake comes out clean.

Let the cake cool in the pan for a couple of minutes, then lift it out and peel off the paper. Transfer to a wire rack to cool completely.

Store in an airtight container and eat within 1 week, or freeze for up to 1 month.

devil's food cake

An unusual, quick, and easy method that produces a very dark cake—yet light and full of flavor.

Chop the chocolate and put it in a heavy saucepan along with the butter, sugar, and syrup. Heat very gently, stirring frequently until melted. Remove the pan from the heat and let cool.

Sift the flour, cocoa, and baking soda into a large bowl and make a well in the center. Pour in the melted chocolate mixture, stir gently, then add the eggs, vanilla extract, and milk. Beat very gently with a wooden spoon until well mixed.

Spoon the mixture into the prepared pans and spread evenly. Bake in a preheated oven at 325°F for 15 to 20 minutes or until just firm to the touch. Remove from the oven and let cool in the pans for 5 minutes, then remove from the pans and transfer to a wire rack to cool completely.

To make the chocolate frosting, first chop the chocolate. Put the milk and sugar in a saucepan and heat gently, stirring frequently until dissolved, then boil rapidly for 1 minute until syrupy. Remove the pan from the heat and stir in the chocolate. When melted and smooth, stir in the butter and vanilla extract. Let cool, stirring occasionally, then beat well until very thick.

Spread one-third of the frosting onto one of the cooled cakes. Set the second layer on top. Spread the rest of the frosting evenly over the top and sides. Leave in a cool spot (not the refrigerator) until set. Store in an airtight container and eat within 5 days. The unfrosted cakes can be frozen for up to 1 month.

3 oz. bittersweet chocolate

1 stick unsalted butter

scant ½ cup dark brown sugar

1 tablespoon golden syrup* or dark corn syrup

1 cup plus 2 tablespoons all-purpose flour

¼ cup unsweetened cocoa powder

½ teaspoon baking soda

2 large eggs, beaten

½ teaspoon real vanilla extract

⅓ cup milk

Chocolate Frosting

2½ oz. bittersweet chocolate

⅔ cup whole milk

½ cup sugar

½ stick unsalted butter, at room temperature

½ teaspoon real vanilla extract

2 cake pans, 7 inches diameter, greased and lined with baking parchment

Makes 1 cake

*Available in larger supermarkets and gourmet food stores.

CHOCOLATE COOKIES

cinnamon chocolate stars

1½ sticks plus
1 tablespoon unsalted butter,
at room temperature

scant ½ cup sugar

1½ cups all-purpose flour

a good pinch of salt

1 teaspoon ground cinnamon

⅓ cup rice flour or cornstarch

2 oz. bittersweet chocolate,
to finish

a star-shaped cookie cutter

several baking trays, greased

Makes 30

Cut these shortbread cookies into any pretty shape, then bake, cool, and dip in chocolate.

Using a wooden spoon or electric mixer, beat the butter until creamy. Gradually beat in the sugar. When the mixture is pale and fluffy, sift in the flour, salt, cinnamon, and rice flour or cornstarch, and mix. When the cookie dough comes together, turn it onto a lightly floured surface and knead lightly and briefly to make a smooth, but not sticky dough. In hot weather, or if the dough feels sticky, wrap it and chill until firm.

Roll out the dough to about ¼ inch thick and cut out shapes with the cookie cutter. Gently knead together the trimmings, then re-roll and cut more stars.

Arrange the stars slightly apart on the prepared baking trays. Prick with a fork and chill for about 15 minutes.

Bake the cookies in a preheated oven at 350°F for 12 to 15 minutes, or until firm and barely colored. Remove from the oven and let cool on the baking trays for a couple of minutes until firm enough to transfer to a wire rack to cool completely.

When the cookies are completely cold, melt the chocolate gently in the top of a double boiler or in a small heatproof bowl set over a saucepan of steaming, not boiling, water. Stir until smooth, then remove the bowl from the heat. Dip the points of the stars in the melted chocolate, then let them set on waxed paper, non-stick parchment, or a wire rack.

When firm, store in an airtight container and eat within 3 days. Undecorated cookies can be frozen for up to 1 month.

chocolate crackles

These cookies crack and spread in the oven—finish them off with a dusting of confectioners' sugar to make them look even more dramatic.

Melt the chocolate gently in the top of a double boiler or in a heatproof bowl set over a saucepan of steaming, not boiling, water, stirring frequently. Remove the bowl from the heat and gradually stir in the butter. In a separate bowl, beat the egg and vanilla extract until frothy using a wire whisk or electric beater. Gradually beat in the sugar, followed by the melted chocolate mixture.

Sift the flour and baking soda into the bowl, then stir it in to make a firm dough. In hot weather, or if the dough seems sticky, wrap and chill it for 15 minutes.

Using your hands, roll the dough into walnut-sized balls. Roll each ball in confectioners' sugar, then arrange on the prepared baking trays, spacing them well apart.

Bake in a preheated oven at 400°F for 10 to 12 minutes or until just firm. Remove the cookies from the oven and let cool on the baking trays for 1 minute, until firm enough to transfer to a wire rack to cool completely.

Store in an airtight container and eat within 1 week, or freeze for up to 1 month.

4 oz. bittersweet chocolate, coarsely chopped

1 stick unsalted butter, diced, at room temperature

1 large egg

2–3 drops real vanilla extract

¾ cup plus 1 tablespoon light brown sugar

1 cup plus 2 tablespoons self-rising flour

½ teaspoon baking soda

about 2 tablespoons confectioners' sugar, for coating

several baking trays, greased

Makes about 28

Only the finest unsweetened chocolate is suitable for this recipe.

bittersweet chocolate butter cookies

2½ oz. unsweetened chocolate, coarsely chopped (preferably with at least 70 percent cocoa solids)

1½ tablespoons superfine or granulated sugar

2 sticks unsalted butter, chilled and diced

¾ cup light brown sugar

1⅔ cups all-purpose flour

½ teaspoon real vanilla extract

2 oz. white or unsweetened chocolate, melted, to decorate

several baking trays, well greased

Makes 30

Put the chocolate and sugar in a food processor and process until they form the texture of sand. Add the diced butter, sugar, flour, and vanilla extract, then process again until the dough just comes together.

Using your hands, form the dough into about 30 walnut-sized balls. Arrange them on the prepared baking trays, spacing them well apart.

Bake the cookies in a preheated oven at 350°F for 10 to 15 minutes, or until they are just firm to the touch and beginning to color around the edges.

Remove from the oven. They are very fragile at this stage, so leave them on the trays for 5 minutes to firm up before transferring to a wire rack to cool.

When the cookies are completely cold, decorate by drizzling with the melted chocolate, using either a fork or a small homemade frosting bag, made from rolled-up waxed paper. Let set.

Store in an airtight container and eat within 4 days. Undecorated cookies can be frozen for up to 1 month, but you may have to crisp them in a warm oven and then let cool, before decorating.

black and white cookies

1 stick unsalted butter,
at room temperature

scant ½ cup light brown sugar

1 large egg, beaten

scant ½ cup self-rising flour

½ teaspoon baking powder

a pinch of salt

½ teaspoon real vanilla extract

1½ cups rolled oats

6½ oz. bittersweet chocolate,
chopped into chunks

several baking trays, greased

Makes about 24

Make chocolate chips by chopping good bittersweet chocolate into large chunks—the flavor is far superior to commercial chocolate chips.

Using a wooden spoon or electric beater, cream the butter until smooth and creamy. Add the sugar and beat until light and fluffy. Gradually beat in the egg, and beat well after the last addition. Sift the flour, baking powder, and salt into the mixture, add the vanilla extract and oats, and stir in. When thoroughly mixed, stir in the chocolate chunks.

Put heaped teaspoons of the mixture, spaced well apart, onto the prepared trays. Bake in a preheated oven at 350°F for 12 to 15 minutes or until golden and just firm. Remove from the oven and let cool on the trays for a couple of minutes, until firm enough to transfer to a wire rack to cool completely.

Store in an airtight container. Eat within 1 week, or freeze for up to 1 month.

Chocolate chip cookies with a difference—the dough is flavored with melted bittersweet chocolate plus chocolate chunks.

giant double-chocolate nut cookies

Melt the 5 oz. chopped chocolate very gently in the top of a double boiler or in a heatproof bowl set over a saucepan of steaming, not boiling, water. Remove the bowl from the heat and let cool.

Meanwhile, beat the butter until creamy using a wooden spoon or electric beater. Add the sugars and beat again until light and fluffy. Gradually beat in the egg and vanilla extract, followed by the melted chocolate.

Sift the flour, salt, and baking powder into the mixture and stir. When thoroughly mixed, stir in the chopped nuts and chocolate chunks.

Put heaped tablespoons of the dough, spaced well apart, on to the prepared baking trays.

Bake in a preheated oven at 350°F for 12 to 15 minutes until just firm. Remove from the oven and let cool on the trays for a couple of minutes until firm enough to transfer to a wire rack to cool completely.

Store in an airtight container. Eat within 1 week, or freeze for up to 1 month.

5 oz. bittersweet chocolate, chopped

7 tablespoons unsalted butter, at room temperature

⅓ cup superfine or granulated sugar

⅓ cup dark brown sugar

1 large egg, beaten

½ teaspoon real vanilla extract

1 cup all-purpose flour

a pinch of salt

½ teaspoon baking powder

2 oz. pecans or walnuts, chopped (about ½ cup)

3½ oz. unsweetened (or white) chocolate, chopped into chunks

several baking trays, greased

Makes 16

BROWNIES
& SNACKS

squillionaire's shortbread

14 oz. can condensed milk, unopened

1 stick unsalted butter, at room temperature

5 tablespoons sugar

1 cup plus 1 tablespoon all-purpose flour

3 tablespoons unsweetened cocoa powder

Chocolate Topping

6 oz. bittersweet chocolate

2 tablespoons unsalted butter, diced

about 2 oz. white chocolate, to finish

a cake pan, 9 inches square and 2 inches deep, greased

Makes 16

To make the filling, put the unopened can of condensed milk in a heavy saucepan and cover with water. Bring to a boil, then simmer without covering the pan, for 3½ hours. Top up the water regularly: the can must always be covered with water. Let the can cool completely before opening. The condensed milk should have become a fudgy, dark, golden caramel.

Meanwhile, to make the chocolate cookie base, beat the butter until creamy, using a wooden spoon or electric beater. Add the sugar and beat until the mixture is light and fluffy. Sift the flour and the cocoa into the bowl and work with your hands to make a smooth dough. Press the dough into the prepared cake pan to make an even layer. Prick well with a fork and chill for 15 minutes.

Bake the chocolate cookie crust in a preheated oven at 350°F for 20 minutes or until just firm and slightly darker around the edges—do not overcook or it will taste bitter. Remove from the oven and let cool in the pan. When completely cold, spread the cold caramel over the top. Chill until firm—1 to 2 hours.

To make the topping, chop the chocolate and melt it gently in the top of a double boiler or in a heatproof bowl set over a saucepan of steaming, not boiling, water. Remove the bowl from the heat and stir in the butter. When smooth, spread it over the caramel and let it set. Melt the white chocolate in the same way, then drizzle it over the top of the bittersweet chocolate, by dipping a fork in the chocolate and letting it drizzle across the shortbread.

Leave overnight until firm before cutting. Store in an airtight container and eat within 1 week. Not suitable for freezing.

three-chocolate squares

Three kinds of chocolate—white, bittersweet, and cocoa—make great treats, good with coffee.

Chop the chocolate, then melt it gently in the top of a double boiler or in a heatproof bowl set over a saucepan of steaming, not boiling, water. Stir occasionally. Remove the bowl from the heat and let cool.

Meanwhile, beat the butter until creamy using a wooden spoon or electric beater. Add the sugar and vanilla extract and beat well. Gradually beat in the egg, followed by the cooled chocolate.

Sift the flour, baking powder, baking soda, and cocoa into a separate bowl. Using a metal spoon, fold the flour mixture into the chocolate batter in 3 batches alternating with the sour cream. When thoroughly mixed, spoon into the prepared cake pan and smooth the surface.

Bake in a preheated oven at 375°F until just firm, 25 to 30 minutes. Remove from the oven and let cool in the pan before removing.

To make the topping, melt the white chocolate in the same way as the bittersweet chocolate above, then stir in the butter. When smooth, spread over the cake and let set. Cut into 16 pieces and store in an airtight container. Eat within 5 days, or freeze for up to 1 month.

2½ oz. bittersweet chocolate

1 stick unsalted butter, at room temperature

¾ cup plus 1 tablespoon light brown sugar

½ teaspoon real vanilla extract

1 large egg, beaten

1⅔ cups all-purpose flour

1 teaspoon baking powder

½ teaspoon baking soda

¼ cup unsweetened cocoa powder

⅔ cup sour cream

White Chocolate Topping

2 oz. good-quality white chocolate, chopped

1½ tablespoons unsalted butter, at room temperature

a cake pan, 8 inches square, greased and lined with baking parchment

Makes 16

fudge brownies

A wonderful version of one of the great American classics.

1¼ sticks unsalted butter
4 large eggs, beaten
1¾ cups light brown sugar
1 teaspoon real vanilla extract
a good pinch of salt
¾ cup unsweetened cocoa powder
1 cup minus 1 tablespoon all-purpose flour
3½ oz. walnut or pecan pieces (scant 1 cup), or chopped white or bittersweet chocolate, or a combination

a cake pan, 9 inches square and 2 inches deep, completely lined with foil

Makes 16

Put the butter in a saucepan and heat gently until melted. Let cool while preparing the rest of the mixture.

Using a wooden spoon, beat the eggs very gently with the sugar until just blended and free of lumps. Stir in the cooled butter and the vanilla extract. Sift the salt, cocoa, and flour together into the butter mixture and gently stir in—do not beat or overmix, or the brownies will become cake-like.

When mixed, fold in the nuts and/or chocolate. Pour into the prepared cake pan and smooth the surface.

Bake in a preheated oven at 325°F for 35 to 40 minutes, or until a skewer inserted midway between the center and the side of the pan comes out clean. The center should be just firm—do not overcook or the brownies will be dry.

Remove from the oven and put the pan on a damp cloth to cool completely.

When cool, lift the brownies out of the pan still in the foil. Remove the foil and cut the brownies into 16 squares.

Store in an airtight container and eat within 1 week, or freeze for up to 1 month.

blondies

These pale-gold brownies are topped with nuts and two kinds of chocolate—dark and white.

Put the butter in a large, heavy saucepan and heat gently until melted. Add the sugar, stir well, then remove the pan from the heat. Let cool for 1 minute, then add the vanilla extract and the eggs, and stir to mix.

Sift the flour, baking powder, and salt into the pan and stir just until thoroughly blended—do not beat or overmix.

Pour the batter into the prepared baking pan and spread evenly. Sprinkle the nuts and chopped chocolate over the top.

Bake in a preheated oven at 350°F for about 25 minutes or until just firm.

Remove from the oven and let cool for a few minutes in the pan, then lift the cake, still in the foil, onto a wire rack to cool completely.

Remove the foil and cut the blondies into 48 squares. Store in an airtight container and eat within 4 days. They can be frozen for up to 1 month, but they will be stickier than freshly baked ones.

1¼ sticks unsalted butter

2 cups light brown sugar

1 teaspoon real vanilla extract

3 large eggs, beaten

2 cups all-purpose flour

1 teaspoon baking powder

a large pinch of salt

2 oz. walnut pieces, coarsely chopped (about ½ cup)

2 oz. good-quality white chocolate, coarsely chopped

2 oz. bittersweet chocolate, coarsely chopped

a roasting or baking pan, 12½ x 9 inches, lined with foil

Makes 48

mocha madeleines

1¼ sticks unsalted butter, at room temperature, diced

3 oz. bittersweet chocolate, coarsely chopped

1 cup minus 1 tablespoon all-purpose flour

2 tablespoons unsweetened cocoa powder

a pinch of salt

1 teaspoon finely ground espresso coffee

4 large eggs

⅔ cup sugar

confectioners' sugar, for dusting

madeleine plaques, twice-buttered*

Makes 30

*Non-stick molds work best. If using ordinary metal molds, brush with 1 coat of melted butter, chill, then brush with a second coat of butter.

A delicate mixture flavored with finely ground coffee.

Put the butter and chocolate in the top of a double boiler or in a heatproof bowl set over a saucepan of steaming, not boiling, water, and melt gently, stirring frequently. Remove the bowl from the heat and let cool.

Meanwhile, sift the flour twice with the cocoa, salt, and coffee, then set aside. Put the eggs and sugar in a separate bowl and beat using an electric beater until the mixture becomes pale and thick—when the beater is lifted out, the mixture should leave a ribbon-like trail on the surface.

Using a large metal spoon, fold the flour mixture into the egg mixture in 3 batches, then carefully fold in the chocolate mixture until all are thoroughly combined (the batter will lose a little bulk).

Put a heaped teaspoon or so of the mixture into each madeleine mold so it is two-thirds full.

Bake in a preheated oven at 375°F for 10 to 12 minutes, or until just firm.

Remove from the oven and let cool for 1 minute, then carefully remove the madeleines from the molds using a butter knife. Transfer to a wire rack to cool completely, then dust with confectioners' sugar.

Store in an airtight container and eat within 1 week, or freeze for up to 1 month.

CHOCOLATE TARTS & PIES

chocolate pear tart

To make the dough, sift the flour into a bowl, then add the diced butter and rub it in with the tips of your fingers until the mixture resembles fine crumbs.

Stir in the sugar, add the egg yolk and water, then bind the mixture together using a butter knife or pastry spatula. If the dough is dry and crumbly, add a little extra water, 1 tablespoon at a time. Without kneading, quickly bring the dough together with your hands to make a soft but not sticky ball.

Alternatively, you may make the dough in a food processor. To do so, put the flour, butter, and sugar in the food processor and process until the mixture resembles fine crumbs. With the machine running, add the egg yolk and water through the feed tube, and process just until the dough comes together.

Wrap the dough and chill it for 20 minutes. Roll out the dough on a lightly floured surface to a circle 11½ inches across, and use to line the tart pan. Chill while preparing the filling.

Put a baking tray in a preheated oven at 400°F to heat up—this helps to make the tart shell crisp.

To make the filling, chop the chocolate, then melt it very gently in the top of a double boiler or in a heatproof bowl set over a saucepan of steaming, not boiling, water. Stir until smooth, then remove the bowl from the heat and let cool.

Meanwhile, using an electric beater or wooden spoon, beat the butter until creamy, then beat in the sugar. When the mixture is light and fluffy, beat in the egg yolks, 1 at a time, beating well after each

1⅓ cups all-purpose flour

1 stick unsalted butter, chilled and diced

2½ tablespoons sugar

1 egg yolk

about 1 tablespoon ice water

vanilla ice cream, to serve

Chocolate Pear Filling

4½ oz. bittersweet chocolate

1 stick plus 1 tablespoon unsalted butter, at room temperature

scant ½ cup sugar

4 large eggs, separated

1⅓ cups ground almonds

2–3 drops real almond extract

a pinch of salt

2 ripe medium pears

a deep, false-bottom tart pan, 9 inches diameter

a baking tray

Makes 1 tart, serves 8

addition. Beat in the cooled chocolate, then stir in the ground almonds and vanilla extract, using a large metal spoon.

In a very clean grease-free bowl, beat the egg whites with the pinch of salt until they form soft peaks. Using a large metal spoon, gently fold them into the chocolate mixture in 3 batches. Gently spoon into the prepared chilled tart shell and spread evenly.

Peel the pears and cut them in half, then scoop out the cores with a melon-baller or pointed teaspoon. Thinly slice the pear halves, leaving the slices attached at the stalk end, so they resemble fans. Arrange the pears on top of the chocolate mixture in a neat pattern.

Remove the heated baking tray from the oven, set the tart pan on it, and return to the oven to bake for 15 minutes. Then reduce the oven temperature to 350°F and bake for about 10 minutes longer, or until just cooked in the center—test by piercing the filling with a skewer, it should come out clean.

Remove from the oven and very carefully unmold the tart. Serve either warm or at room temperature with vanilla ice cream. The tart tastes better the day after baking, though it sinks slightly.

VARIATION

Chocolate Normandy Tart

Substitute crisp, tart apples for the pears and prepare them in the same way. Add ½ teaspoon ground cinnamon to the chocolate filling, and proceed as in the main recipe.

Use just-ripe Comice pears for this rich, not-too-sweet tart.

chestnut and chocolate moneybags

about 10½ oz. phyllo dough, thawed if frozen

1 cup plus 1 tablespoon curd cheese, such as ricotta

3 tablespoons dark brown sugar

2 egg yolks

2–3 tablespoons rum

7 oz. bittersweet chocolate, coarsely grated

4 oz. drained cooked chestnuts (about ¾ cup), roughly chopped (vacuum-packed or canned in light syrup or water)

½ stick unsalted butter, melted, for brushing

confectioners' sugar, for dusting

several baking trays

Makes 12, serves 4–6

To make the filling, beat the curd cheese until softened using a wooden spoon, then beat in the sugar, followed by the egg yolks. Add rum to taste. Using a metal spoon, gently stir in the grated chocolate and the chestnuts.

Remove the pastry dough from the box and cover with a damp cloth until ready to use—the sheets of dough dry out very easily and become unusable.

Put 3 sheets of the pastry dough on top of each other on a counter, and cut into 7-inch squares. Put a heaped tablespoon of the mixture (¹⁄₁₂ of the amount) into the center of each square, gather up the edges, and twist the top to resemble a pastry moneybag. There is no need to dampen the edges of the dough. Repeat to make 12 pastry bags.

Arrange, spaced well apart, on the baking trays and chill for 15 minutes.

Brush the pastry with melted butter, then bake in a preheated oven at 375°F for about 15 minutes, until golden brown. Dust with confectioners' sugar and serve.

Serve warm, at room temperature, or chilled with vanilla ice cream, sour cream, or hot chocolate sauce.

southern deep-dish pecan pie

This delicious pecan pie is made with nuts, chocolate, and bourbon.

To make the dough, put the flour and salt in a food processor. Add the butter and process until the mixture resembles fine crumbs. Add the sugar and process briefly. With the machine running, add the egg yolk and water through the feed tube and process until the dough comes together. Wrap the dough and chill it for 20 minutes until firm.

Roll out the dough to a large circle about 11½ inches across, and use it to line the tart pan. Prick well and chill for about 15 minutes.

To bake the tart shell, place a cut-out circle of parchment paper or wax paper in it, and fill with baking beans. Cook in a preheated oven at 400°F for about 15 minutes or until firm. Remove the paper and beans and return the empty tart shell, still in its pan, to the oven for 5 to 10 minutes, until crisp and golden. Let cool.

To prepare the filling, put the sugar and cream in a heavy saucepan and stir over medium heat until the sugar has melted and the mixture is almost boiling. Remove the pan from the heat and stir in the chocolate. When smooth, add the egg yolks and mix well. Stir over very low heat until the mixture thickens. Remove the pan from the heat and stir in the vanilla extract, bourbon, if using, and nuts. Pour into the prepared pie shell and chill until firm. Serve decorated with white chocolate curls, if using—these are made using a vegetable peeler or grater.

Eat within 3 days. Not suitable for freezing.

1⅓ cups all-purpose flour

a pinch of salt

1 stick unsalted butter, chilled and diced

2½ tablespoons sugar

1 egg yolk

about 1 tablespoon ice water, to bind

Pecan Filling

1 cup plus 1½ tablespoons light brown sugar

1¼ cups heavy cream

2½ oz. bittersweet chocolate, chopped

2 egg yolks

½ teaspoon real vanilla extract

1 tablespoon bourbon (optional)

1⅓ cups pecan halves

shaved or grated white chocolate "curls", to finish (optional)

a deep, false-bottom tart pan, 9 inches diameter

Makes 1 pie, serves 8–10

Amaretti add crunchy texture and nutty taste to this easy recipe.

amaretti chocolate cheesecake

To make the crust, put the melted butter and crushed amaretti crumbs in a bowl and mix, then press onto the bottom of the prepared pan in an even layer. Chill while making the filling.

To make the filling, chop the chocolate and melt it gently in the top of a double boiler or in a heatproof bowl set over a saucepan of steaming, not boiling, water. Remove the bowl from the heat, stir until smooth, then let cool.

Put the cream cheese, eggs, and sugar in a food processor and process until thoroughly mixed. Add the cream and process again until just mixed. With the machine running, add the melted chocolate and amaretto, if using, through the feed tube, and process until smooth.

Spoon the filling into the prepared pan and smooth the surface. Bake in a preheated oven at 325°F for 40 minutes or until firm. Let cool in the oven with the door ajar. When completely cold, put in the refrigerator and chill overnight.

Unclip the pan and remove the cheesecake. Decorate the top with the broken amaretti cookies. Drizzle with the melted chocolate, by dipping a fork in the chocolate and letting it drizzle across the top of the cheesecake.

Store the cheesecake in a covered container in the refrigerator and remove 30 minutes before serving. Eat within 5 days, or freeze for up to 1 month.

½ **stick unsalted butter, melted**

3½ **oz. amaretti cookies, crushed (about 1 cup)**

Chocolate Filling

7 **oz. bittersweet chocolate**

1¾ **cups cream cheese**

2 **eggs**

5 **tablespoons sugar**

scant 1 cup heavy cream

¼ **cup amaretto liqueur (optional)**

To Finish

6 **amaretti cookies, broken**

1½ **oz. bittersweet chocolate, melted**

a springform pan, 8 inches diameter, greased

Serves 12

CHOCOLATE PUDDINGS & CUSTARDS

hot white chocolate pudding

3 oz. white chocolate, chopped

1 stick unsalted butter, at room temperature

½ cup plus 1 tablespoon superfine or granulated sugar

2 large eggs, beaten

1 cup self-rising flour

a pinch of salt

a few drops real vanilla extract

about 3 tablespoons milk

Chocolate Custard

2 cups whole milk

3 tablespoons unsweetened cocoa powder

4 tablespoons superfine or granulated sugar

2 tablespoons cornstarch

2 egg yolks

an ovenproof baking dish, 1 quart, well greased

Serves 4

A special cold weather treat—baked white chocolate sponge pudding, served with hot chocolate custard.

Melt the chopped chocolate in the top of a double boiler or in a heatproof bowl set over a saucepan of steaming, not boiling, water. Remove the bowl from the heat and stir until smooth.

Using a wooden spoon or electric beater, beat the butter until creamy, then gradually beat in the sugar. When the mixture is very light and fluffy, beat in the eggs, 1 tablespoon at a time, beating well after each addition.

Using a metal spoon, carefully fold in the flour and salt, then fold in the melted chocolate, vanilla extract, and enough milk to give the mixture a soft, dropping consistency.

Spoon into the prepared dish—it should be one-half to two-thirds full. Cover loosely with buttered foil and bake in a preheated oven at 350°F for about 35 minutes, or until firm.

Meanwhile, to make the chocolate custard, heat the milk in a saucepan until scalding hot. Sift the cocoa, sugar, and cornstarch into a bowl and mix to a thick paste with the egg yolks and about 1 tablespoon of the hot milk.

Stir in the remaining milk, then return the mixture to the saucepan. Stir over low heat until very hot, thickened, and smooth—do not let it boil. Serve immediately with the chocolate pudding.

chocolate rice pudding

A thoroughly self-indulgent, grown-up version of a traditional English nursery pudding.

Heat the chocolate and milk gently in a saucepan just until melted, stirring occasionally. Remove the pan from the heat and let cool. Put the rice, sugar, and vanilla bean in the buttered baking dish and pour in the chocolate milk.

Stir gently, then bake in a preheated oven at 300°F for about 2½ hours, until the rice is tender and the pudding thickened. Serve warm.

VARIATION

Chocolate Rice Cream

This variation is cooked on top of the stove. Omit the vanilla bean and put the remaining ingredients in a saucepan with 3 green cardamom pods. Bring to a boil, stirring, then simmer for 40 minutes until the rice is soft. Remove the cardamom. Stir in 1 egg yolk and cook for 1 minute. Pour into a large serving dish or individual dishes, let cool, cover, and chill. Serve ice cold, sprinkled with confectioners' sugar or a drizzle of cream.

1 oz. bittersweet chocolate, chopped

2½ cups whole milk

2½ tablespoons short-grain rice

2 tablespoons superfine or granulated sugar

1 vanilla bean*

an ovenproof baking dish, 1 quart, very well buttered

Serves 4

*After using, the vanilla bean can be rinsed carefully, dried, then used again.

rich chocolate soufflé

A wonderfully rich, light, smooth soufflé with a surprise filling.

Brush melted butter inside the soufflé dishes or coffee cups and sprinkle with superfine sugar. Stand them on a baking tray or in a roasting pan.

Put the chocolate and cream into a heavy saucepan. Set over very low heat and stir occasionally until melted. Remove the pan from the heat and stir gently until smooth. Gently stir in the egg yolks, 1 at a time, then half the brandy or liqueur.

Put the 5 egg whites in a very clean, grease-free bowl and beat until stiff peaks form. Sprinkle with the sugar and briefly beat again to make a smooth, stiff meringue. If you over-beat the meringue at this stage it will do more harm than good, and the end result will be less smooth.

The chocolate mixture should be just warm, so gently reheat it, if necessary. Using a large metal spoon, mix in a little of the meringue to loosen the consistency of the chocolate. Pour the chocolate mixture on top of the meringue and gently fold together until thoroughly combined but not over-mixed.

Half-fill the prepared dishes with the mixture. Spoon the remaining brandy or liqueur over the amaretti cookies, then put one in the center of each dish. Add the remaining mixture until the dishes are full almost to the rim.

Bake in a preheated oven at 425°F for 8–10 minutes. Remove from the oven when they are barely set (the centers should be soft and wobble when gently shaken). Sprinkle with confectioners' sugar and serve immediately.

6 oz. bittersweet chocolate, broken into small squares

½ cup plus 1 tablespoon heavy cream

3 eggs, separated, plus 2 egg whites

4 tablespoons brandy or amaretto liqueur

3 tablespoons superfine or granulated sugar, plus extra for sprinkling

4 amaretti cookies

confectioners' sugar, for sprinkling

melted butter, for greasing

4 soufflé dishes, 1¼ cups each, or 4 large coffee cups

a baking tray or roasting pan

Serves 4

chocolate terrine

A velvety smooth finale for a special dinner party–serve this terrine with very strong coffee.

Put the chopped chocolate in the top of a double boiler or in a heatproof bowl along with the cocoa and coffee. Set it over a saucepan of steaming, not boiling, water and melt gently, stirring frequently. Remove the bowl from the heat, stir in the brandy, and let cool.

Meanwhile, put the eggs into the bowl of an electric mixer and beat until frothy. Add the sugar and beat until the mixture is pale and very thick—the beaters should leave a ribbon-like trail when lifted.

In a separate bowl, whip the cream until it holds a soft peak. Using a large metal spoon, gently fold the chocolate mixture into the eggs. When well mixed, fold in the whipped cream.

Spoon the mixture into the prepared pan, then stand the pan in a bain-marie (a roasting pan half-filled with warm water).

Bake in a preheated oven at 325°F for 1 to 1¼ hours, or until a skewer inserted into the center of the terrine comes out clean.

Remove from the oven, let cool in the bain-marie for about 45 minutes, then lift the loaf pan out of the bain-marie and let cool completely.

Chill overnight, then remove from the pan. Serve dusted with confectioners' sugar, if using. Store well wrapped in the refrigerator for up to 5 days.

14 oz. bittersweet chocolate, coarsely chopped

½ cup plus 2 tablespoons unsweetened cocoa powder

3 tablespoons strong espresso coffee

2 tablespoons brandy

6 large eggs, at room temperature

½ cup sugar

1 cup heavy cream, chilled

confectioners' sugar, for dusting (optional)

a loaf pan, 9 x 5 x 3 inches deep, greased and lined with baking parchment

a bain-marie or roasting pan

Serves 8

chocolate brûlée

This pudding is very rich, so serve in small portions.

2¾ cups light cream or light whipping cream

1 vanilla bean, split

10½ oz. bittersweet chocolate, finely chopped

4 egg yolks

½ cup plus 1 tablespoon confectioners' sugar, sifted

about 3 tablespoons superfine or granulated sugar, for sprinkling

8 ramekins (or similar), ⅔ cup each

a bain-marie or roasting pan

Serves 8

Put the cream and the split vanilla bean in a heavy saucepan. Heat until scalding hot but not boiling. Remove the pan from the heat, cover, and let infuse for 15 minutes.

Lift out the vanilla bean and scrape the seeds into the cream using the tip of a small knife.

Stir the chocolate into the cream until melted and smooth. Put the egg yolks and confectioners' sugar in a medium bowl, beat with a wooden spoon until well blended, then stir in the warm chocolate cream. When thoroughly mixed, pour into the ramekins.

Stand the ramekins in a bain-marie (a roasting pan half-filled with warm water) and bake in a preheated oven at 350°F for about 30 minutes or until just firm. Remove the ramekins from the bain-marie and let cool. Cover and chill overnight, or for up to 48 hours.

Sprinkle a little sugar over the tops of the puddings, then put them under a very hot broiler for just a few minutes to caramelize. A warning: if the ramekins are left for too long under the broiler, the chocolate cream will melt. Serve within 1 hour.

sweet
tarts & pies

pastry dough basics

A tart or pie should be a successful combination of a delicious filling and a melt-in-the-mouth pastry.

Pastry dough is most easily made in a food processor, so don't worry if you have hot hands or a less-than-light touch. Just follow the rules; don't overwork or overstretch the dough, or it will be tough and heavy, and don't let the butter turn oily or start to melt as you work the dough, since this makes for soggy, greasy pastry. Use butter straight from the refrigerator, chill the dough before rolling out, then again before baking.

The pastry dough in most of these recipes is made in a food processor. However, to make dough by hand, sift the dry ingredients into a bowl. Add very cold, diced butter, and toss until it is lightly coated in flour. Cut the butter into smaller pieces using a butter knife. Gently rub the butter and flour between your fingertips (not your palms), a little at a time, until the mixture looks like fine crumbs with no large lumps. As you work, lift your hands up to the rim of the bowl to aerate the mixture as it falls back down.

Bind the mixture with ice water, egg yolk, or other liquid using just enough to make a soft dough. If the dough is dry and hard, it will be difficult to use; and if too wet and sticky, it will be tough and heavy when baked. As soon as the dough comes together, lift it out on to a lightly floured surface and gently and briefly knead it to make it smooth and even.

To line a tart pan, roll out the dough on a lightly floured surface to the diameter of the pan plus twice its height. Roll the dough around the rolling pin and lift it over the pan. Gently unroll the dough so it drapes over the pan. Carefully press the dough onto the bottom of the pan and up the sides, so there are no air pockets. Roll the pin over the top of the pan to cut off the excess dough. The sides of the tart shell should stand slightly above the rim, so use your thumbs to press the pastry dough sides upwards to make a neat rim about ¼ inch higher than the pan. Curve your forefinger inside this rim and gently press the pastry dough over your finger so it curves inward to make unmolding easier.

Baking blind produces a crisp tart shell. Prick the pastry dough with a fork, cut a circle of non-stick parchment paper the same size as the pastry dough lining the pan, crumple the paper to make it flexible, open it out, and gently press it into the tart shell to cover the bottom and sides (easier if the dough is chilled and firm). Fill the lined tart shell with ceramic baking beans, dried beans, or uncooked rice to weigh it down. Bake in a preheated oven at 400°F for 15 minutes or until lightly golden and just firm. Carefully remove the paper and beans, then lower the oven temperature to 350°F. Bake for 5 to 7 minutes more, until crisp and lightly golden.

To bake a filled tart, set it on a hot baking tray in the oven—the tart crust will receive an extra boost of heat from the tray and will not become soggy.

FRUIT PIES

lemon meringue pie

1 cup plus 2 tablespoons
all-purpose flour

a pinch of salt

1½ tablespoons superfine
or granulated sugar

1 stick unsalted butter,
chilled and diced

1 large egg yolk, mixed
with 2 teaspoons ice water

Lemon Filling

the juice and grated rind
of 3 medium unwaxed lemons

⅓ cup cornstarch

1¼ cups water

2 large egg yolks

scant ½ cup superfine
or granulated sugar

½ stick unsalted butter, diced

Meringue Topping

3 large egg whites

⅔ cup superfine or
granulated sugar

*a false-bottom
tart pan, 8 inches
diameter*

Serves 6–8

To make the pastry dough in a food processor, put the flour, salt, sugar, and butter in the food processor and process until the mixture resembles fine crumbs.

With the machine running, add the egg yolk and water through the feed tube. Process just until the dough comes together. If there are dry crumbs in the bottom of the bowl, add a little more water, 1 teaspoon at a time, until you have a slightly firm dough.

Alternatively, to make the dough by hand, sift the flour, salt, and sugar into a large bowl, then rub in the diced butter using the tips of your fingers. When the mixture resembles bread crumbs, stir in the egg yolk and water mixture using a butter knife—the mixture should be neither dry and crumbly nor soft and sticky.

If the kitchen is warm, wrap and chill the dough for 15 minutes until firm. Roll out the dough on a lightly floured surface to a circle at least 10 inches across, and line the tart pan with it (see page 71). Prick the bottom of the pie shell all over with a fork, then chill for about 15 minutes.

Bake the pie shell blind as described on page 71 in a preheated oven at 400°F for about 15 minutes or until it is lightly golden and just firm.

Carefully remove the paper and beans, lower the oven temperature to 350°F, and bake for a further 5 to 7 minutes or until the bottom is crisp and lightly golden.

Remove from the oven and let cool while making the filling. Leave the oven at the same temperature.

Put the grated lemon rind and juice in a heatproof bowl. Add the cornstarch and 1 to 2 tablespoons of the water, and stir to make a smooth paste.

Bring the rest of the water to a boil in a medium saucepan, then stir it into the lemon mixture. When thoroughly combined, tip the contents of the bowl back into the saucepan and cook, stirring constantly, until the mixture boils.

Reduce the heat and simmer, stirring frequently, for about 2 minutes or until the mixture is smooth and thick.

Remove the pan from the heat and beat in the egg yolks and sugar, followed by the butter.

Spoon the filling into the pie shell and spread it evenly.

To make the topping, put the 3 egg whites in a non-plastic, spotlessly clean, grease-free bowl and beat until soft peaks form. Beat in the sugar, 1 tablespoon at a time, then beat well to make a stiff, shiny meringue.

Gently spread the meringue over the lemon filling until it is completely covered.

Bake for 15 to 20 minutes in the preheated oven until the meringue is a good golden brown.

Remove from the oven, let cool, then remove from the pan. Serve at room temperature within 24 hours of baking.

A traditional old-fashioned favorite recipe, with a delicious lemon filling made rich and creamy with the addition of butter.

cherry almond pie

1⅔ cups all-purpose flour

a good pinch of salt

½ cup ground almonds

¾ cup plus 1 tablespoon
confectioners' sugar

1½ sticks unsalted butter,
chilled and diced

1 large egg yolk, plus 1 teaspoon
of ice water

sugar, for sprinkling

Cherry Filling

2 tablespoons slivered almonds

1 lb. large black cherries, pitted,
or frozen cherries*

2 teaspoons cornstarch

1–2 tablespoons light brown
sugar, or to taste

a pie dish, 10 inches diameter

a baking tray

Serves 6

*If using frozen cherries, use them straight from the freezer. Sprinkle the slivered almonds over the pie shell and increase the amount of cornstarch to 1 tablespoon.

Put the flour, salt, almonds, and confectioners' sugar in a food processor and process. Add the butter and process until the mixture resembles fine crumbs. With the motor running, add the egg yolk and water through the feed tube and process just until the mixture comes together. If there are dry crumbs and the dough does not come together, add ice water a little at a time. Wrap the dough and chill for 15 minutes until firm enough to roll out.

To prepare the filling, put a slivered almond into the cavity of each cherry. Put in a bowl, add the cornstarch and sugar, and mix well.

Preheat the oven to 400°F and put a baking tray in to heat.

Divide the dough in two, one part slightly smaller than the other. Roll out the small piece on a lightly floured surface to a circle about 11 inches across, and line the pie dish with it, letting the excess drape over the rim. Spoon in the filling, leaving a border around the rim clear and mounding the fruit in the center. Brush the pastry rim with cold water. Roll out the remaining pastry to a circle about 11 inches across. Roll it around the rolling pin, then unroll over the pie, draping it over the filling. To seal, press the top crust firmly onto the dampened rim, then, using a small sharp knife, cut around the edge to cut off the excess dough. Crimp the rim with the back of a fork or your fingertips. Make a steam hole in the center with a sharp knife, and decorate the top with pastry dough leaves made from the excess dough. Put the pie dish on the hot baking tray and cook in the preheated oven for 20 minutes.

Reduce the oven temperature to 350°F, and bake for 10 minutes, or until the crust is golden. Sprinkle with sugar and serve warm or at room temperature. Eat within 24 hours of baking.

apricot crunch

Dried apricots, soaked in orange juice, make
this an easy pie to make with what's on hand.

To make the filling, put the apricots, orange juice, and cinnamon
stick in a non-aluminum saucepan and bring to a boil. Remove the
pan from the heat and let cool completely—preferably overnight.
Drain thoroughly and discard the cinnamon stick.

To make the crust, put the flour, oats, sugar, and ground cinnamon
in a bowl and stir to mix. Add the diced butter and rub in with
your fingertips until the mixture resembles very coarse crumbs.
Add the beaten egg and briefly mix into the crumbs with your
fingers to make pea-sized lumps of dough—do not overmix
or bind the dough together.

Set aside a third of the crust mixture. Scatter the remainder into
the pie dish and press onto the bottom and up the sides, using the
back of a spoon or a fork. Spoon in the drained filling, then lightly
scatter the reserved crust mixture on top.

Bake in a preheated oven at 375°F for about 30 minutes or until
crisp and golden. Serve warm or at room temperature, with ice
cream or fromage frais. Eat within 24 hours of baking.

1 cup all-purpose flour

¾ cup rolled oats

¾ cup light brown sugar

2 teaspoons ground cinnamon

**1½ sticks unsalted butter,
chilled and diced**

1 large egg, beaten

**ice cream or fromage frais,
to serve**

Apricot Filling

1⅓ cups dried apricots

¾ cup unsweetened orange juice

1 cinnamon stick

*a deep-dish pie pan,
9 inches diameter and
about 2 inches deep*

Serves 4–6

Make this pie with your favorite berries, and, in summer, see what berries you can find growing nearby.

apple and berry deep-dish pie

Put the flour, salt, sugar, and butter in a food processor and process until the mixture looks like fine crumbs. With the machine running, gradually add the water through the feed tube to make a soft but not sticky dough. Wrap the dough and chill it.

Gently mix the apples with the berries and a little sugar to taste. If the apples are not juicy, add 1 tablespoon water or lemon juice. Spoon the fruit into the pie dish, heaping it up well in the middle to support the crust, once it's added.

Roll out the dough on a lightly floured surface, to an oval about 3 inches larger than your pie dish all the way around. Cut off a strip of dough about ½ inch wide, and long enough to go around the rim of the dish. Dampen the rim of the dish, and paste on the strip of dough, joining the ends neatly. Dampen the strip of dough, then carefully cover the pie with the rolled-out dough, pressing it onto the dampened strip to seal. With a sharp knife, trim the excess dough and use to decorate the top. Push up the sides of the crust with a small knife, then crimp or flute around the edges. Make a steam hole in the center with a sharp knife.

Bake the pie in a preheated oven at 400°F for about 30 minutes or until the crust is crisp and golden. Sprinkle with sugar and serve warm or at room temperature.

1⅓ cup all-purpose flour

a good pinch of salt

1 teaspoon superfine or granulated sugar

¾ stick unsalted butter, chilled and diced

about 4 tablespoons ice water, to bind

sugar, for sprinkling

Apple and Berry Filling

about 2 lb. crisp tart apples, peeled, cored, and thickly sliced

8 oz. raspberries, mulberries, loganberries, or blackberries

2 tablespoons superfine or granulated sugar, or to taste

1 tablespoon water or freshly squeezed lemon juice (optional)

a deep, oval pie dish, about 9 inches long

Serves 6

FRUIT TARTS

fresh raspberry lattice tart

1½ cups all-purpose flour

½ teaspoon baking powder

scant ½ cup almonds
still in their skins

1 teaspoon ground cinnamon

½ cup superfine or
granulated sugar

1 stick unsalted butter,
chilled and diced

1 egg, plus 1 yolk

sugar, for sprinkling

Raspberry Filling

8 oz. fresh raspberries*
(1½–2 cups)

1–2 teaspoons superfine or
granulated sugar, or to taste

1 rounded teaspoon cornstarch

*a false-bottom tart pan,
8 inches diameter*

a baking tray

Serves 6

*Avoid washing the fruit if possible.
Pick it over well, checking for
blemishes and foreign objects.*

To make the pastry dough, put the flour, baking powder, almonds, cinnamon, and sugar in a food processor and process until the mixture resembles fine sand.

Add the pieces of chilled butter, and process again until the mixture resembles fine crumbs. With the machine running, add the egg and yolk through the feed tube and process to make a soft dough. Wrap and chill the dough for at least 30 minutes until firm enough to roll out.

Roll out the dough fairly thickly on a lightly floured surface to a circle at least 10 inches across. Line the tart pan with it, pressing the dough onto the bottom and sides. Trim off the excess dough and use small pieces of it to repair any tears or holes, saving the remainder to make the strips of lattice crust later. Chill the tart shell and excess dough.

Preheat the oven to 375°F and put a baking tray in to heat.

To make the filling, mix the fresh raspberries with the sugar and cornstarch.

Re-roll the excess dough, and cut it into wide strips.

Spoon the filling into the tart shell, and dampen the top edge of the pastry dough with water. Arrange the strips of dough in a lattice on top, and press the ends onto the top edge to seal.

Set the tart pan on the hot baking tray, and cook in the preheated oven until golden—about 25 minutes. Remove from the oven and sprinkle with sugar.

Serve the tart either warm or at room temperature, within 2 days of baking.

VARIATIONS

Strawberry Liqueur Lattice Tart

To vary the fresh fruit filling, omit the raspberries and sugar, and substitute the same quantity of the finest quality strawberry jam or strawberry compote, mixed with about 2 tablespoons of schnapps or kirsch liqueur, to taste.

Proceed as in the main recipe. The alcohol will cut the sweetness of the jam filling.

Greengage, Apricot, or Cherry Lattice Tart

For these three delicious variations, omit the raspberries and replace with a similar quantity of other fresh fruit. Choose from quartered, pitted, fresh plums; pitted, fresh ripe apricots, cut in half; or pitted, fresh ripe red cherries.

Sprinkle with 2 tablespoons liqueur such as slivovitz (plum brandy) or kirsch, and proceed as in the main recipe.

A fresh fruit version of Linzertorte, the classic tart from the town of Linz in Austria. The rich pastry is flavored and colored with almonds still in their brown papery skins, giving extra taste and texture.

5½ oz. graham crackers (about 22), crushed

3 tablespoons sugar

5 tablespoons unsalted butter, melted

Lemon Cheese Filling

three 8-oz. packages cream cheese (about 3 cups), at room temperature

1 teaspoon real vanilla extract

grated rind of 1 large unwaxed lemon

4 large eggs, beaten

¾ cup sugar

Blueberry Topping

grated rind of ½ large unwaxed lemon

1¾ cups sour cream

½ teaspoon real vanilla extract

1 tablespoon sugar

8 oz. fresh or frozen blueberries (1½–2 cups)

a springform pan, 9 inches diameter, greased

a baking tray

Serves 8–12

blueberry cheesecake tart

A combination of baked lemon cheesecake and blueberry pie—the topping is added toward the end of baking.

To make the crust, mix the cracker crumbs with the sugar and butter. Tip into the prepared pan and press onto the bottom and halfway up the sides, using the back of a spoon or your fingers. Chill the crust while you make the filling.

Put the cream cheese (at room temperature), vanilla extract, and lemon rind in a food processor or electric mixer, and mix at low speed until the mixture is very smooth. Gradually beat in the eggs, increasing the speed as the mixture becomes softer. When thoroughly mixed, beat in the sugar. Pour the filling into the graham cracker crust, then put the pan on a baking tray. Bake in a preheated oven at 350°F for 45 minutes. Remove the cheesecake from the oven and let cool a little—do not turn off the oven.

To make the topping, put the lemon rind, sour cream, vanilla extract, and sugar in a bowl and mix well. Spread the mixture gently over the top of the cheesecake. Top with the blueberries, then bake for 10 minutes more.

Remove from the oven and let cool. Let chill overnight, then remove from the pan. Take the tart out of the refrigerator 30 minutes before serving. Store in a covered container in the refrigerator for up to 4 days.

To avoid a soggy tart shell, cook it thoroughly first, brush with egg white to seal, then cook the filled tart on a preheated baking tray.

lemon tart

1 cup all-purpose flour

a pinch of salt

6 tablespoons unsalted butter, chilled and diced

2 tablespoons sugar

1 large egg yolk

1–2 tablespoons ice water

a little egg white, lightly beaten, for brushing

Lemon Filling

3 large eggs plus 1 yolk

⅔ cup heavy cream

½ cup sugar

grated rind of 2 large unwaxed lemons

freshly squeezed juice of 3 large lemons

a false-bottom tart pan, 9 inches diameter

a baking tray

Serves 6

To make the pastry dough, put the flour, salt, butter, and sugar in a food processor and process until the mixture resembles fine sand. With the machine running, add the egg yolk and water through the feed tube and process just until the dough comes together. Wrap and chill the dough for about 30 minutes.

Roll out the dough on a lightly floured surface to a circle at least 11 inches across. Line the tart pan with it (see page 71). Prick the bottom of the tart shell all over with a fork, then chill for 15 minutes.

Bake the tart shell blind as described on page 71, in a preheated oven at 375°F, then remove from the oven. Do not unmold but immediately brush the bottom with a little egg white, then let cool. Reduce the oven temperature to 325°F and put a baking tray in the oven to heat.

To make the filling, put all the ingredients in a large bowl and beat, by hand, until just mixed. Put the baked tart shell, still in the tart pan, on the hot baking tray, and pour in three-quarters of the filling. Put the tart in the oven, then carefully pour in the remaining filling (this way you avoid spilling the filling as you put the tart in the oven).

Bake for 25 to 30 minutes, or until the filling is firm when the tart is gently shaken. Remove from the oven and let cool before removing from the pan. Serve at room temperature or chilled, and eat within 2 days.

sticky apple tart

To make the pastry dough, put the flour, salt, and butter in a food processor and process until the mixture resembles fine crumbs. With the machine running, add 2 tablespoons ice water through the feed tube—the mixture should come together to make a firm dough. If the dough does not form a ball and is stiff and crumbly, add a little more water. In warm weather, or if the dough seems soft, wrap it and chill for about 20 minutes.

Roll out the dough on a lightly floured surface to a large circle, about 12 inches across, and line the pie dish with it. Press the dough onto the bottom of the dish to eliminate any pockets of air, then trim off the excess using a sharp knife. The dough scraps can be saved for decorations. Decorate the rim of the tart by pressing the dough with the prongs of a fork. Chill the tart shell while making the filling.

Peel, core, and coarsely grate the apple, then mix with the bread crumbs, lemon rind and juice, and the golden syrup or corn syrup. Spoon the mixture into the tart shell—don't press it down to level it, or compress the filling, as you will lose its fluffy texture.

You can decorate the top of the tart filling with decorative dough scraps cut into leaves or apple shapes, if you like. Bake in a preheated oven at 375°F for about 30 minutes or until golden. Serve warm or at room temperature, within 48 hours of baking.

A classic English apple tart—best made with baking apples.

1½ cups all-purpose flour

a good pinch of salt

1⅓ sticks unsalted butter, chilled and diced

2–3 tablespoons ice water, to bind

Sticky Apple Filling

1 large baking apple, such as winesap

3 rounded tablespoons golden syrup* or dark corn syrup

½ cup fresh white bread crumbs

grated rind and freshly squeezed juice of 1 large unwaxed lemon

a pie dish, 10 inches diameter

Serves 6–8

Available in larger supermarkets and gourmet food stores.

fig tart

This is a summery tart that makes a spectacular dinner-party dish. Crisp puff pastry is topped with ripe figs and orange-flavored pastry cream.

Roll out the pastry dough on a lightly floured surface to a circle at least 13 inches across. Line the tart pan with it, letting the excess drape over the rim. Chill the tart shell for about 15 minutes, then trim the excess dough using a sharp knife.

Prick the bottom of the tart shell all over with a fork, then bake it blind as described on page 71, in a preheated oven at 400°F for 12 to 15 minutes or until lightly golden and just firm. Remove the beans and paper, then bake for about 10 minutes more until crisp and cooked through. Remove from the oven and let cool while you prepare the fruit and filling.

Put the halved figs in a bowl, sprinkle with the liqueur, and let macerate for 2 hours or overnight.

To make the pastry cream, put the milk in a saucepan and heat almost to boiling point. Put the egg yolks and sugar in a bowl and beat until light and thick, then beat in the flour. When the mixture is completely smooth, beat in the milk. Return the mixture to the saucepan and cook, stirring constantly, until it boils and thickens. Simmer gently, still stirring, for 2 minutes, then remove from the heat. Sprinkle with a little sugar to prevent a skin forming, and let cool.

When you are ready to serve, fold the whipped cream and liqueur into the pastry cream, and spoon it into the tart shell. Drain the figs and reserve the liqueur. Arrange the fruit on top of the pastry cream filling. Heat the apricot jelly or jam until smooth and very hot, then stir in the reserved liqueur and quickly brush the hot jelly over the figs. Serve immediately.

10½ oz. ready-made puff pastry dough

Fig Topping

12 ripe figs, rinsed, trimmed, and cut in half (or cut in quarters if very large)

3 tablespoons orange liqueur, such as Grand Marnier

4 tablespoons apricot jelly or strained jam, to finish

Pastry Cream Filling

1¼ cups whole milk

4 large egg yolks

¼ cup superfine or granulated sugar

2 tablespoons all-purpose flour

⅔ cup heavy cream, whipped

2 tablespoons orange liqueur, such as Grand Marnier

sugar, for sprinkling

a false-bottom tart pan, 10 inches diameter

Serves 8

apple cinnamon tart

To make the pastry dough, put the flour, salt, and sugar in a food processor and process just until combined. Add the butter and process until the mixture resembles fine crumbs. With the machine running, add the egg yolk and water through the feed tube and process just until the mixture comes together to make a slightly firm dough. If there are dry crumbs, add a little extra water, 1 teaspoon at a time. Wrap and chill the dough for about 20 minutes.

Meanwhile preheat the oven to 400°F. Put a baking tray in the oven to heat up.

Roll out the dough on a lightly floured surface to a large circle at least 13 inches across. Line the tart pan with it, pressing the dough into the pan, and trimming the excess dough using a sharp knife. Chill the tart shell while preparing the filling.

Peel and core the apples, then grate coarsely. Put in a bowl along with the cinnamon, sugar, and dried fruit, and mix well. Pile into the tart shell. Spoon the golden syrup or corn syrup over the filling, then dot with the pieces of butter. Put the tart pan on the hot baking tray and cook in the preheated oven for about 20 minutes.

Remove from the oven and let cool for 1 minute, then remove the tart from the pan. Serve warm. Eat within 2 days of baking.

A good recipe to make with windfall apples, and a change from the usual sliced apple tarts.

1⅓ cups all-purpose flour

a pinch of salt

1½ tablespoons sugar

1 stick unsalted butter, chilled and diced

1 egg yolk mixed with 3 teaspoons ice water

Apple Cinnamon Filling

3 large cooking apples, such as Cortland, about 2 lb. total weight

2 teaspoons ground cinnamon

5 tablespoons sugar, or to taste

3 tablespoons raisins, dried cherries, or dried cranberries

2 tablespoons golden syrup* or corn syrup

2 tablespoons unsalted butter, chilled and diced

a deep, false-bottom tart pan, 9 inches diameter

a baking tray

Serves 6

*Available in larger supermarkets and gourmet food stores.

caramelized pear tart

1⅓ cups all-purpose flour

a pinch of salt

¼ cup ground almonds

2½ tablespoons sugar

7 tablespoons unsalted butter, chilled and diced

1 egg yolk

2–3 tablespoons ice water

Caramelized Pear Filling

1 stick unsalted butter

1 cup sugar

⅓ cup whole blanched almonds

about 4 lb. Bartlett or Comice pears, slightly under-ripe, peeled, cut in half, and cored

a tarte Tatin pan or a skillet with an ovenproof handle, 12 inches diameter

Serves 10

To make the pastry dough, put the flour, salt, ground almonds, and sugar in a food processor and process briefly. Add the butter and process just until the mixture resembles fine crumbs. With the machine running, add the egg yolk and 2 tablespoons ice water through the feed tube. Process just until the mixture binds to make a fairly firm dough. If there are dry crumbs, add a little extra water, 1 teaspoon at a time. Wrap and chill the dough for 20 minutes.

To make the filling, arrange the sliced butter on the bottom of the pan or skillet, to cover the bottom completely. Sprinkle an even layer of sugar over it, then the almonds. Pack the pears into the pan, cut side down, then place over medium heat on top of the stove and cook for 20 minutes or until the butter and sugar have formed a richly golden caramel.

Roll out the dough on a lightly floured surface to a circle to fit the top of the pan. Remove the pan from the heat and let cool for 1 minute to let the bubbling subside. Roll the dough around the rolling pin, then lift the rolling pin over the pan and gently unroll the dough so it covers the filling. Quickly tuck the edges inside the pan. Prick the dough all over with a fork, then bake in a preheated oven at 425°F for 20 minutes or until crisp and golden.

Remove the tart from the oven, leave for 5 minutes, then run a butter knife around the edge to loosen the crust. Place a large plate upside down over the top of the pan and invert the tart so the fruit is uppermost. Serve warm or at room temperature, and eat within 24 hours of baking.

plum tart

A German-style yeast-base tart.

To make the crust, put the flour, salt, and sugar in a bowl and make a well in the center. Crumble the yeast into a small bowl, add the lukewarm milk, and stir until smooth. Pour the liquid into the well in the flour. Add the egg and butter, and gradually work the flour into it to make a soft dough. Knead for 10 minutes until smooth and satiny—if the dough sticks to your fingers, work in extra flour, 1 tablespoon at a time. The dough can be kneaded for 5 minutes using an electric mixer fitted with a dough hook, but do not use a food processor.

Cover the dough with a damp dishtowel and let rise for 1 hour at room temperature.

To prepare the filling, put the plum halves in a bowl, sprinkle with sugar, to taste, and toss well. Set aside.

To make the crumble topping, put the flour and sugar in a bowl and mix. Add the diced butter and rub it into the mixture with your fingertips to make pea-sized clumps of dough. Stir in the nuts and set aside.

Punch down the risen dough with your knuckles, and roll it out to a rectangle about 13 x 10 inches. Transfer the dough to the baking tray and press it out until the tray is covered with the dough. Top with the plums, cut side up, then sprinkle with the crumble topping.

Bake in the preheated oven at 375°F for about 30 minutes or until the bottom is golden, the fruit is tender, and the topping crisp and brown. Serve warm with cream, and eat within 24 hours of baking.

2½ cups white bread flour

½ teaspoon salt

¼ cup sugar

one-half 0.6 oz. cake compressed yeast

¾ cup milk, lukewarm

1 egg, beaten

1½ tablespoons unsalted butter, very soft

cream, to serve

Plum Filling

1 lb. plums, cut in half and pitted

3 tablespoons raw or white sugar, or to taste

Crumble Topping

1 cup all-purpose flour

½ cup light brown sugar

1 stick unsalted butter, diced

1½ cups walnut or pecan pieces

a large baking tray, greased

Serves 8

NUT TARTS & PIES

hazelnut strawberry tart

⅓ **cup hazelnuts**

1⅓ **cups all-purpose flour**

a pinch of salt

scant ½ **cup confectioners' sugar**

1½ **sticks unsalted butter, chilled and diced**

2 large egg yolks

ice cream, to serve (optional)

Strawberry Topping

1 lb. strawberries, raspberries, blueberries, or a combination, plus extra, to serve (optional)

⅔ **cup seedless raspberry jelly**

1–2 tablespoons water

a large baking tray, greased

Serves 8

Toast the hazelnuts in a preheated oven at 350°F until they are a good golden brown—about 8 minutes. If necessary, remove the papery brown husks by rubbing the nuts together in a clean dishtowel. Let cool.

Save about a dozen nuts for decoration. Put the rest in a food processor, add the flour and salt and process until the mixture resembles fine sand. Add the confectioners' sugar and process briefly to mix. Add the diced butter and process until the mixture resembles bread crumbs. With the machine still running, add the yolks through the feed tube—process only until the mixture comes together. Wrap and chill the dough until firm enough to roll out—about 30 minutes.

Roll or press out the pastry dough on the greased baking tray into a circle just over 10 inches across. Flute the edges (decorate by pinching the dough between your fingers). Prick the base all over with a fork, then chill until firm—10 to 15 minutes.

If necessary, reheat the oven to 350°F. Bake the tart shell for about 20 minutes or until firm and light gold (beware—overcooked pastry will taste bitter).

Remove from the oven and let cool until quite firm, then transfer to a serving platter. Decorate the top with the reserved nuts and the strawberries—cut in half, or quartered if large—or other fruit.

Put the raspberry jelly and 1 tablespoon water in a small saucepan and heat. Beat until smooth. Bring to a boil, then brush the hot jelly over the fruit and nuts, completely covering them. Let set.

Serve with ice cream or fruit, if using. Eat within 2 days of baking.

VARIATIONS

Almond Strawberry Tart

Replace the hazelnuts with an equal quantity of blanched whole almonds. First toast the nuts in the oven until golden (take care not to let them burn), then cool. Save a few for decoration, then process the remainder in a food processor along with the flour and salt, and proceed as in the main recipe.

Walnut Berry Tart

Omit the hazelnuts and substitute a similar quantity of walnut pieces—there is no need to toast them in the oven first. Proceed as in the main recipe.

Individual Strawberry Tarts

To make small, individual tarts to serve with tea or coffee, rather than as a dessert, cut the dough into circles about 4 inches in diameter, using a cookie cutter or a small saucer to cut around. Proceed as in the main recipe, baking at the same temperature for about 10 to 12 minutes.

A rich hazelnut cookie base is covered with small berries— strawberries, raspberries, even blueberries will do— then glazed. Simple but glamorous.

pecan fudge pie

Really fresh pecans are essential for this recipe.

To make the dough, put the flour, salt, and butter in a food processor and process until the mixture resembles fine crumbs. With the machine running, add 2 tablespoons water through the feed tube and process just until the dough comes together. If there are dry crumbs in the bottom of the bowl and the dough seems stiff, work in extra water, 1 teaspoon at a time, to make a fairly firm dough.

Alternatively, to make the dough by hand, sift the flour and salt into a large bowl, then rub in the diced butter using your fingertips. When the mixture resembles bread crumbs, stir in enough water to bring the mixture together to make a fairly firm dough.

In warm weather it may be necessary to wrap and chill the dough for 20 minutes before rolling out.

Roll out the dough on a lightly floured surface to a circle at least 10 inches across. Line the tart pan with it, then chill the tart shell.

To make the filling, let the butter cool to lukewarm. Put the eggs, sugar, and vanilla extract in a bowl and beat lightly until frothy, then stir in the melted butter. Sift the flour with the salt and cocoa into the bowl, then fold in using a large metal spoon. When thoroughly mixed, stir in the pecans, then spoon into the pie shell. Bake in a preheated oven at 350°F for about 25 minutes or until just firm. Remove from the oven and let cool, then serve at room temperature. Eat within 3 days of baking.

1 cup plus 2 tablespoons all-purpose flour

a pinch of salt

6 tablespoons unsalted butter, chilled and diced

2–3 tablespoons ice water, to bind

Pecan Filling

1 stick unsalted butter, melted

2 large eggs, beaten

¾ cup plus 2 tablespoons light brown sugar

1 teaspoon real vanilla extract

¼ cup all-purpose flour

a good pinch of salt

⅓ cup unsweetened cocoa powder

1½ cups pecan halves

a false-bottom tart pan, 8 inches diameter

Serves 8

sticky walnut tart

1 cup plus 2 tablespoons all-purpose flour

a good pinch of salt

1½ tablespoons sugar

7 tablespoons unsalted butter, chilled and diced

1 egg yolk, mixed with 2 teaspoons water

vanilla ice cream, to serve

Walnut Filling

1¾ cups walnut halves

6 tablespoons unsalted butter

¼ cup sugar

3 tablespoons chilled honey

⅔ cup heavy cream

a false-bottom tart pan, 8 inches diameter

Serves 8

To make the pastry dough, put the flour, salt, sugar, and butter in a food processor and process until the mixture resembles fine crumbs. With the machine running, add the egg yolk and water through the feed tube and process just until the mixture comes together. Wrap and chill the dough until firm—about 20 minutes.

Turn out the dough onto a lightly floured surface and knead for a couple of seconds until smooth.

Roll out to a circle at least 10 inches across, then line the tart pan with it. Roll the pin over the top of the pan to cut off the excess dough, then neaten the rim with your fingers. Chill for 15 minutes until firm.

Bake the tart shell blind, as described on page 71, in a preheated oven at 375°F. Remove the paper and beans and bake for another 5 minutes to cook the base—it should be firm and just colored.

Remove from the oven and let cool, but leave the oven on.

To make the filling, put the walnuts, butter, sugar, and honey in a heavy skillet, preferably non-stick. Cook, stirring, over low heat until the mixture is a pale straw gold. Stir in the cream and cook for 1 minute until bubbling.

Pour the walnut filling into the tart shell and bake for about 12 minutes or until deep golden brown. Remove the tart from the oven, let cool, then remove it from the pan. Serve at room temperature with vanilla ice cream. Eat within 2 days of baking.

pine nut honey tart

Always use fresh nuts and store opened packages in the freezer.

To make the dough, put the flour, salt, butter, and sugar in a food processor and process until the mixture resembles fine crumbs. With the motor running, add the egg yolk and 1 tablespoon water through the feed tube and process until the dough just comes together. If there are dry crumbs or the dough is stiff, add extra water, 1 teaspoon at a time, to make a just-firm dough. Wrap and chill the dough for 20 minutes.

Roll out the dough on a lightly floured surface to a large circle about 11 inches across. Line the tart pan with it, then chill while preparing the filling.

Heat the oven to 375°F and put a baking tray in the oven to heat.

To make the filling, put the butter in a bowl and beat until smooth and creamy, using a wooden spoon or electric beater, then beat in the sugar and honey until light and fluffy. Gradually beat in the eggs, 1 tablespoon at a time. Stir in the ground almonds, then sift the flour, salt, and baking powder into the bowl and mix gently using a large metal spoon.

Spoon into the pie shell and smooth the surface. Set the tart pan on the hot baking tray and bake for 10 minutes. Gently remove from the oven and scatter the pine nuts on top of the filling. Bake for another 15 minutes or until golden and just firm. Remove from the oven and let cool for 1 minute. Carefully remove from the pan, let cool to room temperature, then serve. Eat within 2 days of baking.

1 cup all-purpose flour

a pinch of salt

6 tablespoons unsalted butter, chilled and diced

2½ tablespoons superfine or granulated sugar

1 large egg yolk

1–2 tablespoons ice water

Pine Nut Filling

½ stick unsalted butter, at room temperature

⅓ cup superfine or granulated sugar

1 tablespoon honey

2 eggs, beaten

⅔ cup ground almonds

2 tablespoons all-purpose flour

a pinch of salt

½ teaspoon baking powder

1 cup pine nuts

a false-bottom tart pan,
8 inches diameter

Serves 6

pear and almond cream pie

To make the pastry dough, put the flour, salt, and butter in a food processor and process until the mixture resembles fine crumbs. With the machine running slowly, pour in the water through the feed tube—it should quickly come together to form a soft but not sticky dough. If there are crumbs, work in extra water, 1 teaspoon at a time. In hot weather it may be necessary to wrap and chill the dough for 20 minutes until firm enough to roll out.

Turn out the dough onto a lightly floured surface. Cut off one-third to make the bottom. Wrap and chill the rest. Roll the piece you've just cut off to a circle at least 12 inches across and line the pie plate with it, pressing the dough into the pan and up its sides, pushing out any air bubbles. Do not trim off the excess.

To make the filling, put the butter and marzipan in a food processor and process until smooth. Add the flour and eggs, and process until very smooth. Spoon the filling into the pie shell, leaving a border around the rim clear. Cut the pear quarters into 2 to 3 vertical slices, ½ inch thick. Put on top of the almond mixture, so there is a slight mound in the middle.

To make the lid, roll out the reserved dough to a circle at least 12 inches across. Dampen the rim of the bottom crust, then cover with the pastry dough lid. Press the edges together firmly to seal. Cut off the excess dough using a sharp knife and cut three steam holes in the top crust.

Bake in a preheated oven at 375°F for about 45 minutes, or until golden brown. Remove from the oven, sprinkle with a little superfine sugar, and let cool. Serve warm or at room temperature, and eat within 2 days of baking.

1⅔ cups all-purpose flour

a pinch of salt

1 stick plus 1 tablespoon unsalted butter, chilled and diced

3 tablespoons ice water, to bind

sugar, for sprinkling

Pear and Almond Cream

1 stick unsalted butter, at room temperature

8 oz. white marzipan (almond paste), broken into pea-sized pieces (about 1 cup)

2 tablespoons all-purpose flour

2 eggs, beaten

4 large slightly under-ripe pears, peeled, quartered, and cored

a deep, metal pie plate, 10 inches diameter

Serves 8

FRENCH & ITALIAN FLAVORS

red fruit croustade

about 8 oz. phyllo dough

about 1 stick unsalted butter

confectioners' sugar,
for sprinkling

Red Fruit Filling

2 tablespoons unsalted butter

1¼ cups fresh bread crumbs

½ teaspoon ground cinnamon
(optional)

3–4 tablespoons superfine or
granulated sugar, to taste

1 lb. mixed red fruit
(blackberries, raspberries,
cherries, red currants, black
currants, or strawberries)

1 teaspoon cornstarch

*a springform pan, 12 inches
diameter, well greased and
sprinkled with sugar*

Serves 8

If necessary, thaw the dough according to the package instructions. Once unwrapped, the dough should be covered with plastic wrap or a damp cloth to keep it from drying out. If it becomes dry and hard, it will crack and become difficult to use. Meanwhile, melt the butter and let cool while preparing the filling.

To make the red fruit filling, heat the butter in a small saucepan, then add the bread crumbs and sauté until golden brown, stirring constantly. Remove the pan from the heat, and stir in the cinnamon and 1 tablespoon sugar. Let cool.

Put the prepared fruit in a bowl, add the cornstarch and the remaining sugar, and toss gently.

Line the bottom of the prepared pan with 2 to 3 sheets of phyllo pastry dough, overlapping where necessary. Let the edges flop over the rim. Brush the dough with melted butter, and sprinkle with a little sugar. Add another 2 to 3 sheets of dough, buttering and sugaring as before. Repeat once more (about half the dough should have been used).

Spread the bread crumb mixture evenly in the pie shell. Add the red fruit filling, but do not press it down. Fold the edges of the phyllo dough over the filling as if wrapping a package. Brush the top with melted butter and sprinkle with sugar.

Lightly brush the remaining sheets of dough with butter, then cut or tear them in half. Crumple each piece of pastry dough like a chiffon scarf, and gently arrange them in a pile on top of the pie. Sprinkle with any remaining sugar, and bake in a preheated oven at 425°F for 15 to 20 minutes or until golden. Remove from the oven, carefully unclip the pan, dust the croustade with confectioners' sugar, and serve.

VARIATIONS

Caramelized Apple Croustade

Replace the red fruit with 2 lb. baking apples such as Cortlands, peeled and thickly sliced. Heat 4 tablespoons butter in a skillet and sauté the apples until golden. Sprinkle with 5 tablespoons sugar and cook until the apples caramelize. Let cool, then proceed as in the main recipe.

Pineapple Croustade

Replace the red fruit with 1 medium pineapple, peeled, cored, and cut into chunks. Heat 4 tablespoons butter in a skillet and sauté the pieces of pineapple until caramelized. Remove the pan from the heat and stir in 2 tablespoons rum. Let cool, then proceed as in the main recipe.

Brands of phyllo dough vary enormously—I use Antoniou, which is excellent, others can be tough and heavy. Ask other cooks for the best local product.

mango tartes tatin

Roll out the pastry dough on a lightly floured surface as thinly as possible. Using a cookie cutter or a saucer as a guide, cut out 6 circles, 4½ inches across. Transfer to the baking trays, prick all over with a fork, and chill while preparing the topping.

Peel the mangoes, and cut the flesh away from the pits. Cut the flesh into strips about ¾ inch thick. Chop the ginger very finely.

Put the butter in a heavy skillet and heat, then add the ginger. Roll the mango slices in sugar, then sauté in the hot butter until golden. Remove the mango to a plate and let cool.

Arrange the mango slices on the mini tart shells, then bake for 10 to 12 minutes in a preheated oven at 425°F or until the pastry is golden.

Decorate with the pistachio nuts and serve immediately. Eat within 24 hours.

Slices of mango are quickly browned in butter and sugar, flavored with ginger, and baked with puff pastry.

10½ oz. ready-made puff pastry dough

3 slightly under-ripe mangoes

2 pieces preserved or candied ginger

6 tablespoons unsalted butter

5 tablespoons superfine or granulated sugar

1 tablespoon shelled pistachio nuts, blanched

2 large baking trays

Serves 6

crème brûlée tart

1⅓ cups all-purpose flour

a good pinch of salt

2½ tablespoons superfine
or granulated sugar

6 tablespoons unsalted butter,
chilled and diced

1 large egg yolk,
plus 1 teaspoon water

4 tablespoons sugar,
for sprinkling

Raspberry Filling

4 oz. fresh raspberries
(about ¾ cup)

4 large egg yolks

5 tablespoons superfine
or granulated sugar

1¾ cups heavy cream

1 vanilla bean, split

½ stick unsalted butter, diced, at
room temperature

*a deep, false-bottom tart pan,
9 inches diameter*

Serves 8

To make the pastry dough, put the flour, salt, and sugar in a food processor and process until just mixed. Add the butter, and process until the mixture resembles fine crumbs. With the machine running, add the egg yolk and water through the feed tube, and process just until the dough comes together. Wrap and chill the dough for 30 minutes.

Roll out the dough on a lightly floured surface to a circle at least 11 inches across, and line the tart pan with it. Chill for 10 to 15 minutes.

Prick the bottom of the pie shell all over with a fork, then bake it blind as described on page 71, in a preheated oven at 400°F for 10 minutes or until golden. Remove the beans and paper, and bake for 15 minutes more, until the base is crisp and golden. Remove from the oven and let cool, but do not remove the pie shell from the pan yet.

To make the filling, first arrange the fruit in the bottom of the cooked pie shell. Put the egg yolks and sugar in a heatproof bowl and beat until very thick and frothy.

Put the cream and vanilla bean in a saucepan and heat until steaming hot, but not boiling. Pour the cream onto the egg mixture in a slow, steady stream, beating constantly. Put the bowl over a saucepan of steaming, not boiling, water and cook slowly, stirring constantly, until thick—about 10 minutes. Remove the bowl from the heat, and take out the vanilla bean. Gradually beat in the butter, then pour the mixture into the pie shell. Let cool, then chill for several hours or overnight, until firm and set.

Sprinkle the tart with sugar, then brown under a preheated hot broiler for a few minutes. Let cool, then chill for 2 to 3 hours before serving. Eat within 24 hours of baking.

torta di ricotta with chocolate pieces

1 cup plus 1 tablespoon
all-purpose flour

3 tablespoons unsweetened
cocoa powder

a pinch of salt

⅔ cup confectioners' sugar

1 stick unsalted butter,
chilled and diced

Ricotta Filling

8 oz. ricotta cheese (about 1 cup)

⅓ cup confectioners' sugar

grated rind of 1 unwaxed orange

1 teaspoon orange liqueur
or real vanilla extract

1 large egg plus 1 yolk

3½ oz. unsweetened chocolate,
coarsely chopped

¼ cup flaked almonds,
for sprinkling

a false-bottom tart pan,
8½ inches diameter

Serves 8

The pie shell is made from a rich chocolate pastry dough, and the light filling has ricotta studded with chunks of dark chocolate.

To make the pastry dough, put the flour, cocoa, salt, and confectioners' sugar in a food processor and process briefly just to mix. Add the pieces of butter and process until the mixture resembles fine sand, then pulse the machine until the dough comes together. Wrap and chill for 20 minutes.

Roll out the dough on a lightly floured surface to a circle at least 11 inches across, and line the tart pan with it. The pastry is quite hard to work, so mend any holes that appear with trimmings, and press the dough together if necessary. Trim any excess dough. Chill the pie shell while preparing the filling.

To make the filling, put the ricotta in a bowl and, using a wooden spoon, beat until creamy. Beat in the confectioners' sugar followed by the orange rind and the liqueur or vanilla extract. When completely mixed, beat in the egg and the egg yolk, then stir in the chocolate. Spoon the mixture into the pie shell and sprinkle with the almonds.

Bake in a preheated oven at 350°F for about 25 minutes or until firm. Remove from the oven and let cool. Remove the tart from the pan and serve at room temperature. Eat within 2 days.

torta di zabaglione

Marsala wine is traditionally used to make zabaglione, but if you find it too sweet in this dish, substitute dry white wine instead.

Toast the almonds in a preheated oven at 350°F for about 10 minutes or until light golden. Let cool. Reduce the oven temperature to 300°F.

To make the crust, put the almonds and confectioners' sugar in a food processor and process until the mixture resembles fine sand.

Put the egg whites in a spotlessly clean, grease-free, bowl. Beat with a hand-held mixer or electric beater until stiff peaks form, then beat in the sugar, 1 tablespoon at a time. Using a large metal spoon, gently fold in the almond mixture and liqueur or almond extract. Spoon the mixture into the pastry bag, and starting in the middle of the pan, pipe a flat coil of the mixture to cover the base of the prepared pan. Then pipe a rim inside the edge of the pan.

Bake the crust in the preheated oven for about 30 minutes until quite hard and golden brown. Remove from the oven and let cool, then unclip the pan and peel off the paper. Put the base on a platter and set aside.

To make the filling, put the yolks, sugar, and wine or Marsala in a heatproof bowl set over a saucepan of boiling water. Beat until the mixture is thick and foamy. Remove the bowl from the heat, and beat until cool. When completely cold, fold in the whipped cream, then spoon the mixture onto the crust. Sprinkle with fresh fruit and serve at once.

1½ cups whole blanched almonds

1 tablespoon confectioners' sugar

2 large egg whites

⅓ cup superfine or granulated sugar

1 teaspoon amaretto liqueur or ½ teaspoon real almond extract

fresh fruit, to finish

Zabaglione Filling

4 large egg yolks*

3 tablespoons superfine or granulated sugar

½ cup dry white wine or Marsala

⅔ cup chilled heavy cream, whipped

a springform pan, 9 inches diameter, greased and lined with non-stick parchment paper

a large pastry bag, fitted with a ½-inch plain nozzle

Serves 6

*See note regarding raw eggs, page 4.

cookies & biscotti

a little indulgence

A homemade cookie is a small luxury. It turns a coffee-break or a midnight snack into a moment of sheer pleasure—a little self-indulgence to warm your own day, or hospitality to brighten someone else's. Making cookies is easy, but a few pointers may be helpful.

Most importantly, you need good ingredients for good results. I always use unrefined, pure cane sugars (except refined confectioners' sugar for decoration), because I find they have a slightly deeper flavor.

I prefer unsalted butter: the taste is better and the cook, rather than the manufacturer, controls how much salt goes in the recipe.

I also prefer medium or large fresh eggs from free-range hens, and I always use them at room temperature, not from the refrigerator.

Organic and stone-ground flours are now sold in most of the bigger supermarkets—I use them because they are healthier and have better flavor.

Nuts should be as fresh as possible: the oils they contain quickly turn rancid when exposed to air, so always store open packages in the freezer.

Use plain chocolate with at least 70 percent cocoa solids. When white chocolate is called for, use best-quality, not children's white chocolate bars.

When using lemon or orange rind, use unwaxed fruit and wash the fruit well before removing the rind.

Best-quality real vanilla extract should always be used. Because vanilla is expensive, some of the extract available is either low-grade or fake and chemical, and so smells and tastes very harsh.

It is worth investing in good tools—they make baking easier and more successful. Accurate measuring cups and spoons are essential (see page 4 for spoon measurements). Electric beaters and food processors don't just save time, they also make complicated recipes easier, less messy, and less exhausting.

Cookies scorch easily, so thin, cheap baking trays can ruin the best recipe and the most careful preparation. Heavy, professional-quality trays or those specially made for cookies are wise investments and last forever.

Good airtight containers are vital for storage—cookies quickly lose their crispness in humid conditions.

An oven thermometer is also very useful. Each oven is an individual—most are temperamental. Learn how yours behaves, how quickly it warms up, how well it retains heat, and where the hot spots are.

Baking times in these recipes are only guidelines, so know your oven, and watch your cookies carefully.

TRADITIONAL COOKIES

oatmeal cookies

Two versions of a classic cookie.

1 cup stone-ground whole-wheat flour

a good pinch of salt

1 teaspoon baking powder

⅔ cup rolled oats

1½ tablespoons sugar

¾ stick unsalted butter, chilled and diced

a cookie cutter, 3 inches diameter

several baking trays, greased

Makes about 16

reduce the sugar in the main recipe to ¾ tablespoon

add ¼ teaspoon curry powder or garam masala*, or 1 teaspoon ground cinnamon or ginger

Makes about 16

*Available in Indian grocery stores and gourmet food stores.

Put all the ingredients in a food processor and process until the dough comes together. (In very cold weather, you may have to work the lumps of dough together with your hands.)

Roll out the dough on a lightly floured surface to about ¼ inch thick. Using a 3-inch cookie cutter, cut the dough into rounds. Knead the trimmings together, re-roll, then cut out more rounds.

Arrange the cookies on the prepared baking trays and prick them well with a fork. Bake in a preheated oven at 375°F for 12 to 15 minutes until they turn color slightly at the edges.

Remove from the oven and let cool on the baking trays for 3 to 4 minutes until firm enough to transfer to a wire rack. Let cool completely, then store in an airtight container. Best eaten within 1 week, or freeze for up to 1 month.

VARIATION

Savory Oatmeal Cookies

Make the dough as in the main recipe, reducing the quantity of sugar and adding the spices. Proceed as in the main recipe, and serve with cheese.

oatmeal raisin cookies

Make these cookies with dried sour cherries or dried cranberries instead of raisins for an unusual and flavorful alternative.

Put the flour, salt, baking powder, and oats in a bowl and mix.

Put the butter, sugar, and vanilla extract in a separate bowl and cream until fluffy, using a wooden spoon or electric beater.

Using your hands or a wooden spoon, gradually work the flour mixture and dried fruit into the creamed butter, then knead the mixture until it comes together. Divide the dough into about 32 equal pieces and roll them into balls with about 1 inch diameter.

Place the balls on the prepared baking trays, allowing room for them to spread, then flatten them slightly with your fingers.

Bake in a preheated oven at 350°F for 10 to 12 minutes, or until golden.

Remove from the oven and let cool on the baking trays for a couple of minutes until firm enough to transfer to a wire rack. Let cool completely, then store in an airtight container. Best eaten within 1 week, or freeze for up to 1 month.

1⅔ cups self-rising flour

a pinch of salt

1 teaspoon baking powder

2⅓ cups rolled oats

2 sticks plus 2 tablespoons unsalted butter, at room temperature

1 cup superfine or granulated sugar

½ teaspoon real vanilla extract

⅓ cup raisins, dried sour cherries, or dried cranberries

several baking trays, greased

Makes about 32

old-fashioned gingersnaps

2⅓ cup self-rising flour

a pinch of salt

1 cup superfine or
granulated sugar

1 tablespoon ground ginger

1 teaspoon baking soda

1 stick unsalted butter

¼ cup golden syrup*
or corn syrup

1 large egg, beaten

several baking trays, greased

Makes 30

**Available in larger supermarkets
and gourmet food stores.*

Sift the flour, salt, sugar, ginger, and baking soda into a large bowl. Put the butter and syrup in a small saucepan and heat very gently, stirring occasionally, until the butter melts. Remove the pan from the heat, let cool until just warm, then pour onto the dry ingredients. Add the egg and mix thoroughly.

Using your hands, roll the dough into 30 walnut-sized balls. Place the balls on the prepared baking trays, allowing room for them to spread, then flatten them slightly with your fingers.

Cook in a preheated oven at 325°F for 15 to 20 minutes or until golden brown. Remove from the oven and leave on the trays for 1 minute to firm up, then transfer to a wire rack to cool completely.

Store in an airtight container and eat within 1 week, or freeze for up to 1 month.

If you like gingersnaps chewy, cook them for about 15 minutes or until just firm. If you prefer them crunchy, leave them in the oven for just a few minutes longer.

A traditional spicy cookie with
sweet candied peel.

spice cookies

⅔ cup all-purpose flour

a pinch of salt

1 teaspoon baking powder

½ teaspoon baking soda

1 teaspoon ground ginger

½ teaspoon apple pie spice

1½ tablespoons superfine
or granulated sugar

2 tablespoons unsalted butter,
chilled and diced

1 tablespoon dried candied citrus
peel, very finely chopped

3 tablespoons golden syrup*
or corn syrup

several baking trays, greased

Makes about 20

**Available in larger supermarkets
and gourmet food stores.*

Sift the flour, salt, baking powder, baking soda, ginger, and apple pie spice into a mixing bowl. (The combination of the two leavening agents is what makes these cookies crack.)

Stir in the sugar. Add the diced butter and rub the mixture together with your fingertips until it resembles fine crumbs. Stir in the candied peel, then the syrup, to make a firm dough. (In cold weather, warm the golden syrup before adding it to the mixture.)

Using your hands, roll the dough into about 20 marble-sized balls. Place the balls on the prepared baking trays, allowing room for them to spread. Bake in a preheated oven at 400°F for about 7 minutes or until golden.

Remove from the oven and let cool on the trays for a couple of minutes until firm enough to transfer to a wire rack. Let cool completely, then store in an airtight container. Best eaten within 1 week, or freeze for up to 1 month.

lemon poppyseed cookies

These crisp, light cookies are great on their own or make a perfect complement to ice creams or fruit salad.

1⅓ cups all-purpose flour

a pinch of salt

½ cup confectioners' sugar

¼ cup superfine or granulated sugar

grated rind of 1 unwaxed lemon

2 teaspoons poppy seeds

1 stick unsalted butter, chilled and diced

1 egg, beaten

several baking trays, lightly greased

Makes about 26

Put the flour, salt, sugars, grated lemon rind, and poppy seeds in a food processor and process until thoroughly mixed. Add the diced butter and process until the mixture resembles fine crumbs. Add the egg and process again until the dough clumps together.

Shape the dough into a log about 3 inches in diameter and wrap it in foil. Chill until hard—at least 2 hours, or up to 1 week. The mixture can be sliced and baked when needed.

When you are ready to bake the cookies, slice the logs into rounds about ¼ inch thick, and place them slightly apart on the prepared baking trays. Bake in a preheated oven at 350°F until the edges are just beginning to turn golden brown—10 to 12 minutes.

Remove from the oven and let cool on the baking trays for a couple of minutes until firm enough to transfer to a wire rack. Let cool completely, then store in an airtight container and eat within 5 days, or freeze for up to 1 month.

SHORTBREAD COOKIES

ginger shortbread cookies

1⅓ cups all-purpose flour

2 oz. fine oat flour (about ½ cup)

1 teaspoon ground ginger

½ teaspoon baking soda

½ cup plus 1 tablespoon light brown sugar

1 piece preserved ginger in syrup, drained and coarsely chopped

1 stick unsalted butter, chilled and diced

a cake pan, 8 inches square, well greased

Makes 9 squares

Three wonderful shortbread recipes: one with a ginger flavor; another with a crunchy, sugary crust—named after Demerara, in Guyana, where some of the world's best sugar is produced; plus a variation using green, unsalted pistachios.

Put the flour, oat flour, ground ginger, baking soda, sugar, and preserved ginger in a food processor and process until the mixture resembles coarse sand. Add the diced butter, then process until you have fine crumbs. Do not overwork the mixture—it should not form a dough.

Set aside 4 tablespoons of the crumbs. Tip the rest of the mixture into the prepared pan and press into an even layer with the back of a spoon. Sprinkle the reserved crumbs on top.

Using a butter knife, score the shortbread into 9 squares. Bake in a preheated oven at 350°F for about 25 minutes or until the cookies are just beginning to turn golden.

Remove the pan from the oven. Cut along the scored lines, but leave the shortbread to cool in the pan before turning out.

Store in an airtight container and eat within 1 week, or freeze for up to 1 month.

demerara shortbread cookies

Put the butter in a bowl and beat until creamy using a wooden spoon or electric beater. Add the sugar and vanilla extract, if using, and beat until the mixture is light and fluffy.

Sift the flour with the rice flour, ground rice, or cornstarch, and the salt, then add to the butter mixture. Work the dough with your hands until it comes together, then knead gently for a few seconds.

Form the dough into a log shape 6 x 3 inches. Roll the log in the demerera sugar until evenly coated. Wrap in foil or waxed paper and chill until firm—about 20 minutes.

Unwrap the log and slice into ½-inch rounds. Arrange slightly apart on the prepared baking trays, prick with a fork, then chill them for about 15 minutes until firm.

Bake in a preheated oven at 350°F for 15 minutes until firm but not colored. Remove from the oven and let cool for a couple of minutes, then transfer to a wire rack to cool completely. Store in an airtight container. Best eaten within 1 week, or freeze for up to 1 month.

VARIATION

Pistachio Shortbread Cookies

Make the dough as in the main recipe, adding the pistachios but omitting the vanilla extract. Roll the dough out on a lightly floured surface to ½ inch thick. Cut into rounds with the cutter, knead the trimmings together, re-roll, and cut more rounds. Omit the demerera sugar. Arrange the rounds slightly apart on the prepared baking trays, then chill for about 15 minutes until firm. Bake as in the main recipe.

2 sticks minus 2 tablespoons unsalted butter, at room temperature

½ cup superfine or granulated sugar

2–3 drops real vanilla extract (optional)

1⅔ cups all-purpose flour

⅓ cup rice flour, ground rice, or cornstarch

a pinch of salt

3–4 tablespoons demerara or other raw sugar, such as turbinado

several baking trays, greased

Makes about 16

omit the vanilla extract and demerera sugar from the above ingredients

add ½ cup shelled pistachio nuts, blanched, dried, and roughly chopped

a cookie cutter, 3 inches diameter

Makes about 14

shortbread cookies 141

chocolate shortbread cookies

This rich, grainy shortbread is perfect served with vanilla ice cream.

2 sticks minus 2 tablespoons unsalted butter, at room temperature

½ cup superfine or granulated sugar

1⅔ cups all-purpose flour

½ cup unsweetened cocoa powder

a good pinch of salt

extra sugar, or confectioners' sugar and cocoa, for sprinkling

a cake pan, 9 inches diameter, greased

Makes 12 triangles

Put the butter in a bowl and beat until creamy and light using a wooden spoon or electric beater. Add the sugar and beat again until fluffy. Sift the flour with the cocoa and salt. Using a wooden spoon or your hands, work the dry ingredients into the butter mixture until the dough comes together. Knead gently for a couple of seconds, then press the dough into the prepared pan to make an even layer.

Cover and chill for 15 minutes. Prick the dough well with a fork and score into 12 triangles with a butter knife.

Bake the shortbread in a preheated oven at 350°F for 15 to 20 minutes—do not let it brown or it will taste bitter.

Remove from the oven, sprinkle with sugar, or confectioners' sugar and cocoa, then cut into sections along the marked lines. Let cool before removing from the pan.

Store in an airtight container and eat within 1 week, or freeze for up to 1 month.

NUT COOKIES

almond crescents

For crunchy texture and intense almond taste, use freshly ground and whole nuts—toasted first—and real almond extract.

1 stick unsalted butter, at room temperature

2–3 drops real almond extract

⅔ cup confectioners' sugar, sifted, plus extra for dredging

a pinch of salt

⅔ cup all-purpose flour, sifted

1½ cups ground almonds

¼ cup whole almonds, lightly toasted, then chopped

several baking trays, greased

Makes about 22

Put the butter and almond extract in a bowl and beat using a wooden spoon or electric beater until light and creamy. Add the sifted sugar and mix slowly, then beat well until fluffy. Add the salt, flour, and ground almonds, then mix thoroughly with a wooden spoon. Mix in the chopped toasted almonds and, if necessary, knead the dough gently, just enough to bring it together.

Do not overwork the dough—it should be quite firm. In warm weather, you may need to wrap and chill the dough for 15 to 20 minutes to harden the dough to the proper consistency.

Using your hands, roll heaped teaspoons of the dough into sausages about 3 inches long, curving each into a crescent. Put them on the prepared baking trays, allowing room for them to spread, then cook in a preheated oven at 325°F for 15 to 18 minutes or until firm. They should still be pale, with only the tops slightly browned.

Remove from the oven and let cool on the trays for about 2 minutes, then dredge with confectioners' sugar. Transfer the crescents to a wire rack to cool completely.

Store in an airtight container and eat within 1 week. This recipe does not freeze successfully.

pecan lace cookies

These delicate cookies are perfect
to serve after dinner with sherbet or
with cups of strong, black, coffee.

Melt the butter very gently in a small saucepan, then let it cool
while you prepare the other ingredients.

Put the nuts, sugar, and flour in a food processor and process until
the nuts are finely ground. With the machine still running, pour in
the cream and butter through the feed tube. Process until you
have a soft dough.

Put heaped teaspoons of the mixture on the prepared baking
trays, allowing room for them to spread. Flatten them with a fork,
then bake in a preheated oven at 350°F for 7 to 9 minutes or until
they turn golden brown with slightly darker edges.

Remove from the oven and let cool on the baking trays. Store the
cookies in an airtight container and eat within 4 days. They do not
freeze well.

½ **stick unsalted butter**

1 **cup chopped pecans or walnuts**

½ **cup superfine or granulated sugar**

3 **tablespoons all-purpose flour**

2 **tablespoons heavy cream**

*several baking trays, lined with
waxed paper*

Makes about 24

espresso walnut squares

1 cup all-purpose flour

a pinch of salt

¾ cup light brown sugar

7 tablespoons unsalted butter, chilled and diced

1 teaspoon baking powder

1 egg, beaten

3 tablespoons very strong espresso coffee, cold

1 tablespoon milk

½ cup walnut pieces

a cake pan, 8 inches square, greased and lined with baking parchment or waxed paper

Makes 16 squares

For the best flavor, make the strongest possible espresso coffee, then let it cool before using.

Sift the flour, salt, and sugar into a large bowl. Add the diced butter and rub it in with your fingertips until the mixture resembles coarse crumbs. Set aside 4 tablespoons of the mixture. Add the baking powder to the rest and mix well. Put the egg, coffee, and milk in a small bowl and mix, then stir it into the flour mixture. When thoroughly mixed, add three-quarters of the nuts. Spoon the mixture into the prepared pan and smooth the surface.

Mix the remaining nuts with the reserved crumbs and sprinkle over the top.

Bake in a preheated oven at 350°F for 20 to 25 minutes or until golden brown and firm to the touch.

Remove from the oven, let cool for 1 to 2 minutes, then run a butter knife around the edges of the pan to loosen the cake before carefully turning it out onto a wire rack.

Leave until completely cold before cutting into 16 squares. Store in an airtight container and eat within 4 days, or freeze for up to 1 month.

mocha macaroons

These cookies should be made with the freshest nuts, best-quality chocolate, and good, strong espresso-style coffee.

3 oz. unsweetened chocolate, chopped

2 egg whites

1 cup superfine or granulated sugar

1½ cups ground almonds

1 tablespoon strong brewed espresso coffee

sliced, split, or slivered almonds, to decorate

several baking trays, well greased or lined with non-stick baking parchment

Makes 18

Put the chopped chocolate in the top of a double boiler or in a heatproof bowl set over a saucepan of steaming, not boiling, water, and melt gently. Remove the bowl from the heat and stir until smooth. Let cool slightly.

Put the egg whites in a separate bowl and beat using an egg beater or electric beater until they form stiff peaks. Gradually beat in the sugar, then fold in the almonds, coffee, and melted chocolate.

When well mixed, put heaped teaspoonfuls of the mixture on the prepared baking trays allowing room for them to spread. Smooth into circles about 3 inches across, then sprinkle with the almonds.

Bake in a preheated oven at 300°F for about 25 minutes or until the macaroons are firm.

Remove from the oven, let cool slightly, then lift them off the greased tray (or baking parchment). Transfer them to a wire rack and let cool completely.

Store in an airtight container and eat within 1 week. The macaroons do not freeze well.

Use sugar-free peanut butter in this recipe, or the cookies will be much too sweet.

peanut butter and jelly sandwich cookies

1 generous cup crunchy unsweetened peanut butter

¾ cup superfine or granulated sugar

2–3 drops real vanilla extract

1 large egg, beaten

about 4 tablespoons raspberry jam or red currant jelly, for the filling

several baking trays, well greased

Makes about 12 sandwiches

Put the peanut butter and sugar in a bowl and beat well with a wooden spoon. Beat in the vanilla extract and the beaten egg. The dough should be very stiff.

Divide the dough into 24 pieces and roll them into balls with your hands. Place the balls on the prepared baking trays, allowing room for them to spread, then flatten them with a fork.

Bake in a preheated oven at 350°F for 12 to 15 minutes or until golden brown. Remove the cookies from the oven and leave them on the baking trays for a few minutes to firm up, then transfer to a wire rack to cool completely.

Sandwich pairs of cookies together with a little jam or jelly.

Store in an airtight container and eat within 1 week. The cookies can be frozen for up to 1 month, but they must be frozen without the jam or jelly filling.

NOTE: This recipe is suitable for people on gluten-free diets, and for serving during Passover.

macadamia white chocolate crumbles

1⅓ cups all-purpose flour

a pinch of salt

½ teaspoon baking powder

1½ sticks unsalted butter, at room temperature

½ cup superfine or granulated sugar

1 egg, lightly beaten

½ teaspoon real vanilla extract

5½ oz. good-quality white chocolate, coarsely chopped

3 oz. unsalted macadamia nuts, coarsely chopped (about ⅔ cup)

several baking trays, lightly greased

Makes about 24

An elegant combination of white nuts, white chocolate, and a white cookie mixture.

Sift the flour, salt, and baking powder into a bowl.

Put the butter and sugar in a separate bowl and beat until light and fluffy, using a wooden spoon or electric beater.

Beat the egg into the butter mixture and, when thoroughly mixed, stir in the flour mixture using a large metal spoon. When no streaks are visible, stir in the vanilla, chocolate, and macadamias.

Put tablespoons of the mixture on the prepared baking trays, allowing room for them to spread. Bake in a preheated oven at 350°F for 10 to 12 minutes or until firm but not colored. Let the cookies cool on the trays for 1 minute, then transfer to a wire rack to cool completely.

Store in an airtight container and eat within 5 days. These cookies do not freeze well.

Walnuts make wonderful cookies, but pecans or hazelnuts will also work well in this recipe.

walnut cookies

½ cup walnut pieces, chopped

7 tablespoons unsalted butter, at room temperature

⅓ **cup superfine or granulated sugar**

⅓ **cup raw or white sugar**

1 large egg, beaten

½ **teaspoon real vanilla extract**

1⅔ **cups self-rising flour**

several baking trays, greased

Makes 24

Walnuts can sometimes be very bitter, and can also turn rancid very quickly when exposed to air, so taste one first before using them in this recipe.

Beat the butter until soft and creamy, using a wooden spoon or electric beater. Gradually beat in the sugars and continue beating for another 2 minutes.

Beat in the egg a little at a time, then stir in the vanilla extract, flour, and chopped nuts. Work the mixture with your hands until it comes together into a firm dough. Again using your hands, roll the dough into 24 walnut-sized balls.

Put the balls on the baking trays, allowing room for them to spread, then flatten them with a fork. Bake in a preheated oven at 350°F for about 10 minutes or until the cookies are golden and firm.

Remove the cookies from the oven, leave on the baking trays for a couple of minutes to firm up, then transfer to a wire rack to cool completely.

Store in an airtight container and eat within 1 week, or freeze for up to 1 month.

AROUND
THE WORLD

almond biscotti

These twice-baked biscotti from Tuscany are served after dinner with fresh fruit and a glass of sweet Vin Santo wine for dipping and sipping.

1 cup blanched almonds

1⅔ cups all-purpose flour

½ cup plus 1 tablespoon vanilla sugar, if available, or regular sugar

¾ teaspoon baking powder

2 large eggs, plus 1 egg yolk

½ teaspoon real almond extract or vanilla extract

a baking tray, greased

Makes about 20

Put the almonds on a heatproof dish or tray and toast in a preheated oven at 350°F for 10 to 12 minutes or until lightly browned. Let cool, then coarsely chop ½ cup of the nuts and set aside. Leave the oven on.

Put the remaining nuts in a food processor or blender and grind to a fine powder.

Put the ground almonds in a bowl, add the flour, sugar, and baking powder, and mix. Make a well in the center. Beat the eggs with the egg yolk and the almond or vanilla extract, and pour into the well in the flour. Gradually work the flour mixture into the eggs, then add the chopped almonds. Knead very well to bring the dough together—do not add any extra liquid.

Divide the dough in half and shape each piece into a flat log about 10 x 2½ x ¾ inch. Place the logs well apart on the baking tray. Bake at 350°F for about 25 minutes or until golden and firm to the touch. Remove from the oven and let cool for about 5 minutes. Reduce the oven temperature to 325°F.

Transfer the logs to a cutting board. Using a serrated knife, carefully cut them diagonally into slices ¾ inch thick. Arrange the slices, cut side up, on the baking tray and bake for a further 10 to 12 minutes or until golden and crisp.

Remove the biscotti from the oven, leave on the tray for 5 minutes to firm up, then transfer to a wire rack to cool completely. Store in an airtight container and eat within 2 weeks.

cinnamon and raisin biscotti

Traditional biscotti, flavored with fennel seeds, are served as a digestif. This recipe is a modern variation.

Put the almonds on a heatproof dish or tray and toast in a preheated oven at 350°F for 10 to 12 minutes until lightly browned. Let cool and leave whole.

Put the egg, sugar, and vanilla extract in a bowl and whisk by hand or with an electric beater, until very thick and pale (ribbons of mixture should trail from the beater as you lift it out of the bowl). Sift the flour, baking powder, salt, and cinnamon onto a piece of waxed paper, then sift again into the bowl with the egg mixture. Stir until thoroughly mixed, then stir in the raisins and almonds. Turn the dough out onto the prepared baking tray and shape it into a flat log about 10 x 2½ x ¾ inch.

Bake the log in a preheated oven at 350°F for 20 to 25 minutes or until golden brown. Remove from the oven, let cool for about 5 minutes, or until firm, then transfer to a cutting board. Reduce the oven temperature to 325°F.

With a serrated knife, carefully cut the log diagonally into slices about ½ inch thick. Arrange the slices on the tray, and bake again for 10 to 15 minutes or until golden. Remove the biscotti from the oven and let cool on the tray for 5 minutes, then transfer to a wire rack to cool completely. Store in an airtight container and eat within 2 weeks.

⅓ cup whole blanched almonds

1 large egg

½ cup superfine or granulated sugar

1 teaspoon real vanilla extract

¾ cup all-purpose flour

½ teaspoon baking powder

a pinch of salt

¾ teaspoon ground cinnamon

¼ cup raisins

a baking tray, well greased

Makes about 20

Tuiles are the perfect accompaniment to ice cream, creamy desserts, or fruit salads.

orange tuiles

Put the egg whites in a spotlessly clean, grease-free, non-plastic bowl. Beat slowly at first using an egg beater or electric beater, then increase the speed until the egg whites form stiff peaks. Gradually beat in the sugar, then the cooled melted butter, and then the sifted flour. If you use an electric beater, keep it on low speed.

Gently stir in the grated orange rind and the liqueur, if using.

Spoon 1 teaspoon of the batter onto a prepared baking tray and spread it into a thin disc about 4 inches across. Bake it in a preheated oven at 350°F for about 5 minutes or until it turns a very pale gold.

Remove from the oven and, using a spatula, immediately loosen it from the tray and drape it over a rolling pin. It will harden very rapidly into a U-shape. Remove and set aside. Once you have the knack, bake the tuiles 2 at a time.

Store in an airtight container, and eat within 2 days—humidity or dampness makes them uncurl, so store with care. These cookies are not suitable for freezing.

2 egg whites,
at room temperature

⅔ cup superfine
or granulated sugar

½ stick unsalted butter,
melted and cooled

½ cup all-purpose flour, sifted

grated rind of
1 unwaxed orange

1 teaspoon orange liqueur
(optional)

several baking trays, greased

Makes about 18

danish cookies

A hint of cinnamon makes these delicate, lacy cookies an excellent match for ice cream, sherbets, or mousses.

1½ sticks unsalted butter

2 cups rolled oats

1 cup plus 2 tablespoons superfine or granulated sugar

2 eggs, beaten

1 tablespoon all-purpose flour

2 teaspoons baking powder

1 teaspoon ground cinnamon

several baking trays, well greased or lined with non-stick baking parchment

Makes about 24

Put the butter in a medium saucepan and melt gently. Remove the pan from the heat and stir in the rolled oats. When thoroughly mixed, add the sugar, eggs, flour, baking powder, and ground cinnamon, and mix well.

These cookies are best baked in batches of three. (Cook the batches on one baking tray while the other is cooling down).

Space 3 mounds—each about 1 heaped teaspoon of the mixture—on a baking tray, allowing room for them to spread.

Bake in a preheated oven at 350°F for 5 to 7 minutes or until golden brown.

Remove from the oven and, using a spatula, immediately lift the baked cookies off the sheet and let cool upside down on a wire rack. Repeat the process until all the mixture is used.

These cookies quickly lose their crispness in damp or humid conditions, so store carefully in an airtight container and eat within 4 days. They do not freeze well.

irish whiskey fingers

Soak the fruit in whiskey the night before baking—Irish whiskey gives the best flavor, but Scotch is very good too.

Using a vegetable peeler, pare off the rind of the lemon and put it in a small bowl. Add the golden raisins, then pour the whiskey over them. Cover the bowl tightly and leave overnight.

Using a wooden spoon or electric beater, beat the butter until creamy. Beat in the sugar and continue beating until the mixture is very light and fluffy. Beat in the egg yolks one at a time.

Remove the lemon rind from the whiskey mixture, then add the golden raisins and whiskey to the cake batter, carefully folding them in with a metal spoon.

In another bowl, whisk the egg whites until they form stiff peaks, then fold them into the batter in 3 batches alternating with batches of the flour, until the egg whites and flour are used up.

Spoon the batter into the prepared pan and smooth the surface. Sprinkle with the raw or white sugar, then bake in a preheated oven at 350°F for about 25 minutes, or until just firm to the touch.

Remove the cake from the oven, let it rest in the pan for about 5 minutes, then carefully unmold it onto a wire rack. Let cool completely, then cut into 10 long slices.

Store in an airtight container and eat within 1 week, or freeze for up to 1 month.

1 unwaxed lemon

1 cup golden raisins

⅓ cup whiskey

1 stick plus 1 tablespoon unsalted butter, at room temperature

⅔ cup superfine or granulated sugar

2 large eggs, separated

¾ cup self-rising flour

1–2 tablespoons raw or white sugar

a cake pan, 8 inches square, greased and lined with non-stick baking parchment or waxed paper

Cuts into 10 fingers

sablés

Put the flour, salt, confectioners' sugar, and diced butter in a food processor and process until the mixture resembles fine sand. Add the egg yolks and vanilla extract, and process again until the mixture comes together as a firm dough. Take it out of the food processor, wrap, and chill it for 15 minutes.

Roll out the chilled dough on a lightly floured surface to about ¼ inch thick. Cut out rounds with the cookie cutter and space them slightly apart on the baking trays.

Knead the trimmings together, roll again, cut more rounds, and arrange them on the trays. Brush the cookies very lightly with beaten egg, then chill for 15 minutes.

Brush again with the egg glaze, prick all over with a fork, then mark with the prongs to make a neat pattern.

Bake the cookies in a preheated oven at 350°F for 12 to 15 minutes or until golden brown. Remove from the oven, leave on the baking trays for a few seconds to firm up, then carefully transfer to a wire rack to cool completely.

Store in an airtight container and eat within 1 week, or freeze for up to 1 month.

For authentic flavor, make these vanilla-scented French cookies with best-quality unsalted butter.

1⅓ cups all-purpose flour

a pinch of salt

¾ cup confectioners' sugar

1 stick plus 1 tablespoon unsalted butter, chilled and diced

3 egg yolks

½ teaspoon real vanilla extract

1 egg, beaten, to glaze

a fluted cookie cutter, 3½ inches diameter

several baking trays, greased

Makes about 10

STICKS & BARS

sour cream cardamom squares

1⅔ cups self-rising flour

½ teaspoon baking soda

a pinch of salt

¼ teaspoon ground cardamom

1½ sticks unsalted butter,
at room temperature

1¼ cups superfine
or granulated sugar

3 large eggs

⅔ cup sour cream

confectioners' sugar, for dusting

*a cake pan, 8 inches square,
greased and lined with non-stick
baking parchment or waxed paper*

Makes 9

Sift the flour with the baking soda, salt, and ground cardamom, then set aside.

Using a wooden spoon or electric beater, beat the butter until creamy. Gradually beat in the sugar and continue beating until the mixture is very light and fluffy. Add the eggs 1 at a time, beating well after each addition. Using a large metal spoon, fold in the flour mixture in 3 batches, alternating with the sour cream.

Spoon the batter into the prepared cake pan and smooth the surface. Bake in a preheated oven at 350°F for 45 minutes or until golden brown and firm to the touch.

Remove from the oven, loosen the edges with a butter knife, then turn onto a wire rack to cool completely. When cold, cut into 9 squares and dust with confectioners' sugar.

Store in an airtight container and eat within 1 week, or freeze for up to 1 month.

If using whole cardamoms, crack the pods, remove the seeds, and crush them with a mortar and pestle.

mincemeat crumble

Sift the flour, salt, and cinnamon into a bowl. Rub in the diced butter with your fingertips until the mixture resembles fine crumbs. Stir in the sugar, diced apple, dried fruit, and peel. Put the egg and milk in a separate bowl and mix. Add this to the flour mixture and stir to make a soft dough.

Transfer the dough to the the prepared pan and smooth the surface. Sprinkle with the raw or white sugar.

Bake in a preheated oven at 400°F for about 20 minutes or until firm and golden. Remove from the oven, let cool for 1 minute, then cut into 9 squares.

Let cool completely, then store in an airtight container. Eat within 4 days, or freeze for up to 1 month.

VARIATION

Dried Fruit, Pineapple, and Apricot Crumble

Omit the apple and substitute 1 cup of one of the luxury dried fruit mixtures containing pineapple and apricot, that are often available around holiday time.

Crisp, tart apples are best for this quick and easy crumble.

1½ **cups self-rising flour**

a pinch of salt

½ **teaspoon apple pie spice**

6 **tablespoons unsalted butter, chilled and diced**

3½ **tablespoons raw or white sugar**

1 **medium apple, peeled, cored, and diced**

¾ **cup mixed dried fruit, and peel**

1 **large egg**

¼ **cup milk**

1–2 **tablespoons raw or white sugar, for sprinkling**

a cake pan, 8 inches square, greased

Makes 9

pecan spice bars

7 tablespoons unsalted butter, at room temperature

3 tablespoons golden syrup* or corn syrup

1 large egg

1¼ cups self-rising flour

a pinch of salt

¼ teaspoon grated nutmeg

½ teaspoon apple pie spice

¼ teaspoon ground ginger

1 cup coarsely ground pecans

1½ tablespoons milk

Spicy Pecan Topping

2 tablespoons flour

2 tablespoons light brown sugar

¼ teaspoon grated nutmeg

¼ teaspoon grated ginger

2½ tablespoons unsalted butter, chilled and diced

¼ cup pecan halves

a cake pan, 8 inches square, greased and lined with non-stick baking parchment or waxed paper

Makes 15

*Available in larger supermarkets.

An excellent combination of moist sponge cake and crunchy topping of nuts and spices.

Using a wooden spoon or electric mixer, beat the butter until light and fluffy. Beat in the syrup, then gradually beat in the egg.

Sift the flour with the salt and spices, then stir into the butter mixture. Add the ground pecans and milk and stir well. Spoon the mixture into the prepared pan and smooth the surface.

To make the topping, put the flour, sugar, and spices in a bowl and mix. Rub in the diced butter with your fingertips to make small clumps of dough. Stir in the pecans.

Sprinkle the clumps over the base mixture in the pan, then bake in a preheated oven at 350°F for 25 to 30 minutes until firm to the touch.

Remove the cake in its paper lining from the pan. Let cool, then slice into 15 pieces. Store in an airtight container and eat within 1 week, or freeze up to 1 month.

Use only genuine maple syrup for a more intense flavor.

new england maple syrup pecan bars

Put the butter, sugar, and syrup in a medium saucepan, and heat gently, stirring occasionally, until the sugar has dissolved. Remove the pan from the heat, then stir in the oats and nuts, and mix well.

Transfer the mixture to the prepared pan and spread evenly, pressing down lightly. Using a sharp knife, score the mixture into 10 rectangles.

Bake in a preheated oven at 300°F for 25 to 30 minutes or until golden.

Remove from the oven, and cut along the scored lines. Do not remove the bars from the pan until they are completely cold. Store in an airtight container and eat within 1 week, or freeze for up to 1 month.

VARIATIONS

Dried Fruit, Chocolate, Spice, or Nut Bars

Omit the pecans and maple syrup, and replace with 1 tablespoon corn syrup and one of the following: 2 tablespoons raisins, 3 tablespoons chocolate pieces, 1 teaspoon ground ginger, ¼ cup each of chopped dates and walnut pieces, ¼ cup chopped almonds and a few drops of almond extract, or ¼ cup chopped mixed nuts together with ¼ cup soft dried apricots.

1¼ sticks unsalted butter

⅔ cup light brown sugar

1 tablespoon maple syrup

2½ cups rolled oats

½ cup pecans, coarsely chopped

a cake pan, 8 inches square, well greased

Makes 10

tangy lemon bars

¾ cup all-purpose flour

a pinch of salt

⅓ cup confectioners' sugar

7 tablespoons unsalted butter, chilled and diced

3 drops real vanilla extract

Lemon Topping

2 eggs

¾ cup plus 2 tablespoons sugar

grated rind and freshly squeezed juice of 1 large unwaxed lemon

1 tablespoon all-purpose flour

½ teaspoon baking soda

confectioners' sugar, for dusting (optional)

a cake pan, 8 inches square, well greased

Makes 12

Put the flour, salt, and confectioners' sugar in a food processor and process to mix. Add the butter and the vanilla extract and process until the mixture comes together to make a firm dough.

Press the dough into the bottom of the prepared pan to make an even layer. Prick well with a fork and, if the weather is very warm, chill for 15 minutes.

Bake in a preheated oven at 350°F for 12 to 15 minutes or until firm and slightly golden but not browned.

Remove from the oven and let cool in the pan while making the topping.

Using an electric beater or mixer, beat the eggs in a bowl until frothy. Gradually beat in the sugar and continue until the mixture is thick and foamy. Beat in the lemon rind and juice, then the flour and baking soda. Pour the mixture over the cooled cake and bake for 20 to 25 minutes or until golden brown.

Remove from the oven and let cool in the pan, then divide into 12 rectangles. Dust with confectioners' sugar before serving, if you like. Store in an airtight container and eat within 4 days. This recipe does not freeze well.

A crisp, buttery cake with a sticky topping and a sharp citrus tang.

flavored
breads

homemade bread

With such exotic, ever-changing variety on the supermarket shelves, why make bread? It saves money, of course, and has a taste and texture worlds away from even the best you can buy. You need no special talent—just flour, yeast, salt, water, a baking tray, an oven, and some time.

Much of the flavor in homemade bread comes from quality flours. Spelt, for instance, is higher in protein, with more vitamins and minerals than ordinary flours. Whole-wheat flour with added bran makes a light, textured loaf with nutty flecks. White bread flour can be mixed with other flours, such as rye, to lighten them. Stone-ground whole-wheat flour makes a chewy, coarse-textured loaf. Other ways of flavoring dough comes from additions such as poppy seeds, cheese, herbs, or walnuts.

Rising agents include dried yeasts and fresh compressed yeast. Wrapped in plastic, compressed yeast can be refrigerated for 1 week or frozen for 1 month. When you make bread, dried yeast is mixed with flour: compressed yeast with liquid, usually water.

The amount of salt is crucial. Add too little and the dough will rise too fast, then collapse; while too much will inhibit the effectiveness of, or even kill the yeast.

The quantity of liquid needed to form the dough depends on the condition of the flours, the type of flavorings, and even the weather. The ideal texture is soft but not sticky, add extra flour or water as necessary.

Thorough kneading is vital. It develops gluten, the substance in the flour that acts as scaffolding to support the bubbles of carbon dioxide from the yeast. It also ensures that the yeast is evenly distributed through the dough so it rises uniformly. Knead by hand or in a mixer fitted with a dough hook, but not in a food processor.

When dough is left to rise uncovered, it forms a dry crust, which results in hard lumps in the baked loaf. So always cover your rising dough with a damp cloth or a large plastic bag. Too little rising time produces a heavy, small loaf. Too much is even worse: dough seriously distended by too long or too quick a rise will collapse in the oven.

Preheating the oven is important. A hot oven kills yeast quickly and prevents over-rising. All ovens are different, so check shelf positions in your handbook and take my cooking times as guidelines, particularly with convection ovens. To test whether a loaf is cooked, unmold it and knock on the bottom with your knuckles: it should sound hollow. If it doesn't, replace and bake for 5 minutes more before testing again.

Baked bread should be removed from the tray or pan and cooled on a wire rack to help form a good crust. For best results, slice bread only when it's completely cool.

MEDITERRANEAN BREAD

bacon and walnut fougasses

4 tablespoons olive oil, plus extra for brushing and greasing

3 oz. bacon, finely chopped (about ½ cup)

⅔ cup walnut pieces, coarsely chopped

4⅔ cups unbleached white bread flour, plus extra for dusting

2 teaspoons sea salt

0.6 oz. cake compressed yeast, crumbled*

1¼ cups lukewarm water

1 egg, beaten

several baking trays, greased

Makes 8 pieces

To use active dry yeast, add 1 package to the flour when you add the salt.

Heat 1 tablespoon olive oil in a skillet, add the bacon, and sauté until golden and crisp, but not hard. Drain on paper towels, then mix well with the walnuts.

Put the flour and salt in a large bowl, mix well, then make a well in the center. Put the yeast and water in a small bowl, and cream to a smooth liquid. Tip the liquid into the well in the flour, then mix in the egg and the remaining olive oil. Gradually work in the flour to make a soft but not sticky dough. If there are crumbs in the bottom of the bowl, add water, 1 tablespoon at a time, until the dough comes together. If the dough sticks to your fingers, work in more flour, 1 tablespoon at a time.

Lift out the dough and transfer it to a lightly floured surface. Knead thoroughly for 10 minutes or until the dough feels smooth, very elastic, and silky.

Put the dough in a lightly oiled bowl and turn the dough over so the entire surface is lightly coated with oil.

Cover with a damp cloth and let rise at room temperature until doubled in size—about 1½ hours. Uncover, punch down the dough, then turn it out onto a lightly floured surface. Knead in the bacon and nuts until evenly distributed.

Divide the dough into 8 equal parts. Using a rolling pin, roll each piece into an oval about 8½ x 5 x ½ inch. Using a sharp knife, cut about 8 slits in a herringbone pattern in each oval. Put them on the prepared baking trays, spacing them well apart. Lightly cover the bread with a damp cloth and let rise at cool to normal room temperature until doubled in size—about 45 minutes.

Uncover, lightly brush with oil, then bake in a preheated oven at 400°F for 15 to 20 minutes or until golden brown. Remove from the oven and transfer to a wire rack to cool.

VARIATION

Salami Fougasses

Omit the bacon and walnuts. Skin a 4 oz. piece of saucisson sec or salami, chop finely, and add after the first rising. Proceed as in the main recipe.

These attractive, individual loaves come from Provence where, these days, they are made plain or flavored with charcuterie, olives, herbs, or even candied fruit. Use top-quality bacon, such as *poitrine fumée* or dry-cured, thick-cut, and smoked.

focaccia with rosemary and sea salt

This dough has three risings. For an open, light texture, don't overload with olive oil.

Put the yeast and half the water in a small bowl and cream to a smooth liquid. Add 3 tablespoons oil and the remaining water. Add the salt, chopped rosemary, and half the flour. Beat into the liquid with your hand. When mixed, work in enough of the remaining flour to make a soft but not sticky dough.

Turn out the dough onto a lightly floured surface and knead for 10 minutes until very smooth and silky (or for up to 5 minutes at low speed in a mixer fitted with a dough hook). Put the dough in a lightly oiled bowl and turn the dough over so the entire surface is coated with oil. Cover with a damp cloth and let rise at cool to normal room temperature until doubled in size—about 2 hours.

Uncover, punch down the dough, then turn it out onto a lightly floured surface. Shape it into a rectangle. Press into the bottom of the pan, pushing into the corners, and patting out to make an even layer. Cover with a damp cloth and let rise as before until almost doubled in height—45 minutes to 1 hour.

Flour your fingertips and press into the risen dough to make dimples ½ inch deep. Cover with a damp cloth and let rise again until doubled in height—about 1 hour. Uncover the dough and press rosemary sprigs into the dimples and fill them with olive oil. Sprinkle with sea salt and bake in a preheated oven at 425°F for 20 to 25 minutes or until golden brown. Remove from the oven, lift the loaf out of the pan, and transfer to a wire rack to cool.

0.6 oz. cake compressed yeast, crumbled*

1⅛ cups water, at room temperature

6–7 tablespoons extra virgin olive oil, plus extra for greasing

2 teaspoons sea salt

2 tablespoons finely chopped fresh rosemary, plus extra sprigs

about 3⅓ cups unbleached white bread flour, plus extra for dusting

2 teaspoons coarse sea salt

a roasting or baking pan, about 14 x 10 inches, greased

Makes 1 loaf

*To use active dry yeast, add 1 package with the chopped rosemary. Put all the liquid in the bowl at once and proceed with the recipe.

Two variations on the main focaccia recipe.

focaccia with pancetta

Additional Ingredients

4–6 oz. pancetta or bacon (⅔–¾ cup)

about 3 tablespoons extra-virgin olive oil

sea salt and coarsely ground black pepper

a roasting or baking pan, about 14 x 10 inches, greased

Makes 1 loaf

Follow the recipe on page 188, omitting the fresh rosemary and sea salt.

During the first rising, broil the pancetta or bacon, and discard any rind and small pieces of bone. Drain on paper towels and let cool, then chop finely and sprinkle with coarsely ground black pepper.

Punch down the risen dough and knead in the pancetta or bacon. Roll out the dough to fit the pan, then proceed as in the main recipe, drizzling with olive oil to fill the dimples and sprinkling with sea salt and coarsely ground black pepper. Bake, then let cool, as in the main recipe.

cherry tomato focaccia with basil

Follow the recipe on page 188, omitting the fresh rosemary and sea salt.

Cut the tomatoes in half and strip the leaves from a large bunch of fresh basil. Just after making the dimples, push a basil leaf into each hollow, then half a tomato, cut side up. Cover the dough and let rise as before until doubled in height—about 1 hour.

Drizzle with olive oil to moisten the tomatoes and sprinkle with sea salt and pepper. Bake, then let cool, as in the main recipe.

Additional Ingredients

1 cup ripe fresh cherry tomatoes

a large bunch of fresh basil

¼ cup extra-virgin olive oil

sea salt and freshly ground black pepper

a roasting or baking pan, about 14 x 10 inches, greased

Makes 1 loaf

The longer the olives marinate in the flavored oil, the better. For a sharper taste, use green olives.

italian ciabatta with olives and thyme

1½ cups black olives, preferably kalamata, pitted

⅔ cup virgin olive oil

a strip of unwaxed lemon rind

3 teaspoons chopped fresh thyme leaves

4⅔ cups unbleached white bread flour, plus extra for sprinkling

two 0.6 oz. cakes compressed yeast, crumbled*

2 cups cold water

2½ teaspoons sea salt

2 baking trays, well greased

Makes 2 loaves

*This recipe is not successful made with active dry yeast.

Put the olives in a bowl with the olive oil, lemon rind, and thyme. Cover and let marinate for 3 to 4 hours or overnight.

Put 3½ cups flour in a large bowl and make a well in the center.

Put the yeast and ½ cup water in a small bowl and cream to a smooth liquid. Pour the liquid into the well in the flour, then add the remaining water. Mix to a sticky dough, almost like batter.

Cover with a damp cloth and let rise at normal room temperature for 3 to 4 hours. It should grow to about 3 times its original size. Check occasionally to make sure the dough has not stuck to the cloth. Punch down the risen dough.

Strain the olives, discard the lemon zest, and reserve the oil. Mix the oil and salt into the dough, then gradually work in the remaining flour to make a soft, sticky dough. Cut the dough in half and put 1 portion in another bowl. Mix half the olives into each portion.

Cover with damp cloths and let rise as before until doubled in size—about 1 hour.

Tip the dough onto a baking tray and shape into 2 rectangles, 1 inch thick. Push the olives back into the dough, sprinkle with flour, and let rise uncovered at room temperature until doubled in size—about 1 hour. Bake in a preheated oven at 425°F for about 30 minutes or until the loaves are brown and sound hollow when tapped underneath. Remove from the oven and transfer to a wire rack to cool.

olive oil bread

Put the flour and salt in a large bowl, mix, then make a well in the center.

Put the yeast and 3 tablespoons of the water in a small bowl and cream to a smooth liquid. Pour into the well in the flour, then add most of the remaining water. Quickly mix the flour into the liquid, then pour in the oil and continue mixing until the dough comes together. Gradually add the rest of the water, if necessary—the dough should be fairly soft, but should hold its shape and not stick to your fingers.

Turn out the dough onto a lightly floured surface. Knead thoroughly for 10 minutes until the dough is elastic and silky smooth. Put the dough in a lightly oiled bowl and turn the dough over so the entire surface is lightly coated with oil. Cover with a damp cloth and let rise at cool to normal room temperature until doubled in size—about 2 hours.

Turn out the dough onto a floured surface. Do not punch down or knead, but gently shape the dough into a 22-inch long sausage. Join the ends to make a ring. Transfer to the prepared baking tray, cover with a damp cloth, and let rise as before until almost doubled in size—about 1 hour.

Uncover the loaf, dust with flour, and bake in a preheated oven at 450°F for 10 minutes. Reduce to 375°F and bake for another 20 minutes or until it sounds hollow when tapped underneath. Remove from the oven and transfer to a wire rack to cool.

6⅔ cups unbleached white bread flour, plus extra for dusting

3½ teaspoons sea salt

0.6 oz. cake compressed yeast, crumbled*

about 2¾ cups water, at room temperature

½ cup extra-virgin olive oil

vegetable oil, for greasing bowl

a large baking tray, lightly greased

Makes 1 large loaf

To use active dry yeast, add 1½ packages to the flour with the salt, then proceed with the recipe.

For this Italian-style loaf, use well-flavored olive oil and good-quality, stone-ground, organic flour.

SPICES & SEEDS

saffron braided loaf

1 heaped teaspoon
saffron threads

⅔ cup warm water

5 cups white bread flour, plus
extra for dusting

1 tablespoon sea salt

1 teaspoon sugar

2 tablespoons unsalted butter,
chilled and diced

0.6 oz. cake compressed yeast,
crumbled*

1¼ cups skim milk,
at room temperature

1 egg, beaten

vegetable oil, for greasing bowl

1 egg beaten with a
good pinch of salt, to glaze

a large baking tray, greased

Makes 1 large loaf

*To use active dry yeast,
add 1 package to the flour with
the salt and sugar, then proceed
with the recipe.*

Put the saffron on a heatproof plate or tray and toast in a preheated oven at 350°F, without burning, for 10 to 15 minutes. Crumble it into a bowl, then add the warm water, stir, cover, and let soak overnight.

Next day, put the flour, salt, and sugar in a large bowl and mix. Add the diced butter and rub it in with your fingertips until the mixture looks like bread crumbs. Make a well in the center, then pour in the saffron and its soaking water.

Put the yeast and milk in a small bowl, and cream until smooth. Stir in the egg, then pour it into the well in the flour. Work the mixture to form a fairly firm, soft dough. If any dry crumbs remain, work in some extra milk, 1 tablespoon at a time. If the dough sticks to your fingers, work in some extra flour, 1 tablespoon at a time.

Turn out the dough onto a lightly floured surface and knead thoroughly for 10 minutes (or 5 minutes at low speed in a mixer fitted with a dough hook). The dough should be very elastic and silky smooth. Put into a lightly oiled bowl and turn the dough over so the entire surface is lightly coated with oil. Cover with a damp cloth and let rise at normal room temperature until doubled in size—about 1½ hours.

Uncover the dough, punch it down with your knuckles, then turn it out onto a floured surface. The dough should be pliable but not soft, and it should hold its shape well. If not, knead in a little more flour.

Divide the dough into 3 or 4 equal pieces, and braid as described below. Cover with a damp cloth and let rise at a cool temperature until almost doubled in size—1 to 1½ hours. Don't let it over-rise or become too soft in a warm place or it will spread.

Uncover the braided loaf and brush the top with egg glaze. Bake in a preheated oven at 450°F for 15 minutes until golden. Reduce the oven temperature to 400°F and bake for 20 to 30 minutes until it sounds hollow when tapped underneath. Remove from the oven and transfer to a wire rack to cool.

To make a three-strand braid

Using your hands, roll 3 pieces of dough into ropes 16 inches long. Put the 3 ropes on the baking tray, then braid loosely together. Avoid overstretching the dough. Tuck the ends under to give a good shape.

To make a four-strand braid

Using your hands, roll 4 pieces of dough into ropes 13 inches long and 1 inch thick. Pinch them firmly together at one end, then arrange vertically in front of you, side by side, slightly apart, with the join at the top. Run the far-left strand under the 2 middle ones, then back over the last strand it went under. Run the far-right strand under the twisted 2 in the middle, then back over the last strand it went under. Repeat until all the dough is braided. Pinch the ends together at the bottom. Transfer to a baking tray, tucking the ends under to give a neat shape.

Saffron gives a rich gold color and a deep, aromatic flavor to bread dough. The longer the saffron is soaked, the better.

vanilla challah

Made to celebrate the Jewish sabbath, this rich, sweet bread can be flavored with honey, saffron, or spices.

Put the milk, sugar, and vanilla bean in a small saucepan and heat until just steaming. Cover and set aside until the milk cools to lukewarm.

Remove the bean and scrape the seeds into the milk. Put the yeast and the milk in a small bowl and cream to a smooth liquid.

Put the flour and salt in a large bowl and mix. Make a well in the center, pour the yeast liquid, butter, and eggs into the well, then mix. Work in the flour to make a soft but not sticky dough. If too dry, add lukewarm water, 1 tablespoon at a time. If sticky and soft, work in flour, 1 tablespoon at a time. Turn the dough out onto a floured surface and knead for 10 minutes until silky and elastic.

Return to the washed and lightly oiled bowl and turn the dough until the entire surface is lightly coated with oil. Cover with a damp cloth and let rise in a cool spot until doubled in size—1½ to 2 hours.

Punch down the dough, cover, and let rise as before—about 45 minutes. Punch down again and knead in the bowl for 1 minute. Let rest in the bowl, covered with the cloth, for 5 minutes.

Divide and braid the dough as described on page 199. Brush with 2 thin coats of egg-yolk glaze and bake in a preheated oven at 425°F for 10 minutes. Remove from the oven, glaze again, then reduce the heat to 375°F and bake for 30 minutes or until the loaf is golden brown and sounds hollow when tapped underneath. Remove from the oven and transfer to a wire rack to cool.

1 cup skim milk

2 tablespoons sugar

1 vanilla bean, split lengthwise

0.6 oz. cake compressed yeast, crumbled*

5 cups unbleached white bread flour, plus extra for dusting

2½ teaspoons sea salt

¾ stick unsalted butter, melted and cooled

3 eggs, beaten

vegetable oil, for greasing bowl

1 egg yolk beaten with a pinch of salt, to glaze

a large baking tray, greased

Makes 1 loaf

*To use active dry yeast, add 1 package to the flour with the salt and sugar, then proceed with the recipe.

A loaf with the distinctive taste of rye without the heavy texture—stone-ground rye flour will produce the best flavor.

rye and caraway loaf

3 cups unbleached white bread flour, plus extra for dusting

1¾ cups rye flour

2 tablespoons caraway seeds

1 tablespoon sea salt

0.6 oz. cake compressed yeast, crumbled*

2 cups cold water

a baking tray, greased

Makes 1 large loaf

*To use active dry yeast, mix 1 package with the flours, seeds, and salt. Add the water and proceed with the recipe.

Put the two flours, caraway seeds, and salt in a large bowl and mix. Make a well in the center.

Put the yeast and a little of the water in a small bowl, and cream to a smooth liquid. Pour this into the well in the flour along with the rest of the water, then mix in the flour to make a soft but not sticky dough. If too sticky, add extra white flour, 1 tablespoon at a time. If there are dry crumbs in the bottom of the bowl and the dough is stiff and hard to work, add extra water, 1 tablespoon at a time.

Turn out the dough onto a lightly floured surface and knead thoroughly for 10 minutes. Return to the bowl, cover with a damp cloth, and let rise until doubled in size—about 2 hours.

Uncover the dough, punch down with your knuckles, then turn out onto a lightly floured surface. Knead lightly into an oval. With the edge of your hand, make a crease down the middle, then roll the dough over to make a sausage. Put the seam underneath so the top is smooth and evenly shaped. Place on the baking tray, cover with a damp cloth, and let rise until doubled in size—about 1 hour.

Uncover the loaf and slash the top several times with a very sharp knife. Bake in a preheated oven at 400°F for 15 minutes until golden, then reduce the oven temperature to 375°F and bake for a further 20 to 25 minutes until the loaf sounds hollow when tapped underneath. Remove from the oven and transfer to a wire rack to cool.

chile pepper bread

A mixed-flour loaf, speckled with dried chile flakes. Wonderful with smoked salmon and cream cheese—the combination of hot, cold, and savory is irresistible.

Put the dried chile flakes, flours, and salt in a large bowl and mix. Make a well in the center. Put the yeast and a little of the water in a small bowl and cream to a smooth paste.

Pour the yeast paste and the rest of the water into the well. Gradually work the flour into the liquid to make a soft but not sticky dough. If it sticks to your hands, add extra white flour, 1 tablespoon at a time. If there are dry crumbs in the bowl and the dough is stiff and hard to work, add water, about 1 tablespoon at a time. Turn out the dough onto a lightly floured surface and knead for 10 minutes until very elastic and pliable. Return to the bowl, cover with a damp cloth, and let rise at cool to normal room temperature until doubled in size—about 2 hours.

Uncover, punch down the risen dough with your knuckles, then turn out onto a lightly floured surface and shape to fit your pan. Put the dough in the pan and tuck under the ends to make a neat shape (the top of the dough should be halfway up the sides of the pan). Cover and leave at cool to normal room temperature until the dough rises just above the rim of the pan—about 1½ hours.

Uncover and bake in a preheated oven at 450°F for about 15 minutes. Reduce the oven temperature to 400°F and cook for 25 to 30 minutes or until the loaf sounds hollow when removed from the pan and tapped underneath. Transfer the loaf to a wire rack to cool.

2–3 teaspoons dried chile flakes, or to taste

2 cups white bread flour, plus extra for dusting

1½ cups stone-ground whole-wheat bread flour, plus extra for dusting

1½ cups stone-ground rye flour

1 tablespoon sea salt

0.6 oz. cake compressed yeast, crumbled*

2 cups water, at room temperature

a loaf pan, 2 lb., greased

Makes 1 large loaf

*To use active dry yeast, mix 1 package with the chile flakes, flours, and salt. Add all the liquid at once and proceed with the recipe.

poppyseed loaf

A speckled, airy bread—great with soups and for making sandwiches.

Put the poppy seeds, flour, and salt in a large bowl and mix. Add the diced butter and rub it in with your fingertips until the mixture resembles fine crumbs. Stir in the sugar and make a well in the center.

Put the yeast and a little of the milk in a small bowl and cream to a smooth liquid. Pour into the well in the flour along with the egg and remaining milk.

Work the flour into the liquid to make a soft but not sticky dough. Turn out onto a lightly floured surface and knead thoroughly for 10 minutes. Return to the bowl, cover with a damp cloth, and let rise at cool to normal room temperature until doubled in size—1½ to 2 hours.

Uncover, punch down the risen dough, then turn out onto a lightly floured surface. Knead it smooth for 1 minute, then pat into a rectangle the length of the pan and about ½ inch thick. Roll up the dough like a jelly roll from one short end. Pinch the seam with your fingers to seal, then put the dough into the pan, seam side down, tucking under the ends to make a neat shape (the top of the dough should be halfway up the sides of the pan). Cover with a damp cloth and let rise at room temperature until doubled in size—about 1 hour.

Uncover, brush the top with milk, and bake in a preheated oven at 450°F for 15 minutes. Reduce the oven temperature to 400°F and bake for 20 to 30 minutes, until the loaf sounds hollow when removed from the pan and tapped underneath. Transfer the loaf to a wire rack to cool.

¼ cup poppy seeds

4⅓ cups unbleached white bread flour, plus extra for dusting

2 teaspoons sea salt

½ stick unsalted butter, chilled and diced

1½ tablespoons sugar

0.6 oz. cake compressed yeast, crumbled*

1⅓ cups skim milk, at room temperature, plus extra for brushing

1 egg, beaten

a loaf pan, 2 lb., greased

Makes 1 large loaf

*To use active dry yeast, add 1 package to the flour with the salt and poppy seeds, then proceed with the recipe.

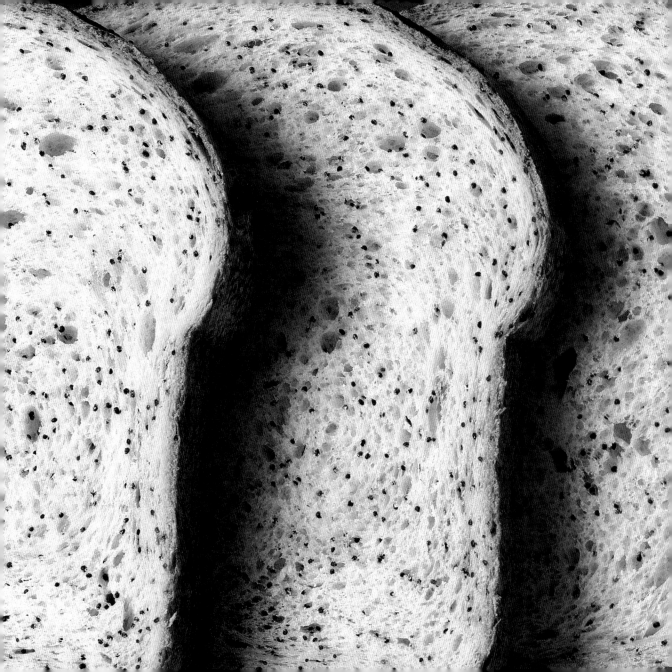

SPECIAL GRAINS

molasses mixed-grain pumpernickel

1½ cups stone-ground rye flour

1 cup coarse stone-ground whole-wheat bread flour

⅔ cup spelt flour

⅓ cup barley flour

⅓ cup fine oat flour

⅓ cup buckwheat flour

⅔ cup white bread flour, plus extra for dusting

2 teaspoons sea salt

1½ tablespoons dark brown sugar

0.6 oz. cake compressed yeast, crumbled*

1½ cups water

¼ cup molasses

1 tablespoon vegetable oil

a loaf pan, 2 lb., greased

Makes 1 large loaf

*To use active dry yeast, mix 1½ packages with the white flour. Put the other flours, salt, and sugar in a bowl, make a well, pour in the water and add yeast mixture.

Put the flours, salt, and sugar in a large bowl and mix. Make a well in the center.

Put the yeast and a little of the water in a small bowl, and cream to a smooth liquid. Stir in the rest of the water, then pour it into the well in the flour.

Mix some of the flour into the liquid to make a thick, smooth batter in the well. Sprinkle a little flour over the batter to prevent a skin forming, then cover and leave the bowl for 30 minutes or until the batter looks bubbly.

Stir the molasses and oil into the batter, then gradually work in the rest of the flour to make a soft, slightly sticky dough. It will seem heavier and more difficult to work than other bread doughs, but if it is dry or too hard to work, you may need to add a little extra water, 1 tablespoon at a time. If it seems wet or too sticky, add a little extra white flour, 1 tablespoon at a time.

Turn out the dough onto a floured surface and knead thoroughly for about 5 minutes. Cover the dough with an upturned bowl, let rest for about 5 minutes, then knead for a further 5 minutes. Return the dough to the bowl, cover with a damp cloth, and let rise at normal room temperature until doubled in size—about 3 hours.

Uncover, punch down the risen dough, then turn out onto a lightly floured surface and knead for 1 minute. Shape the dough into a loaf to fit the pan, then put it in the pan, pushing it into the corners—the top of the dough should be halfway up the pan. Cover with a damp cloth and let rise at normal room temperature until the dough reaches the top of the pan—1½ to 2 hours.

Uncover and bake in a preheated oven at 400°F for about 40 minutes or until the loaf is dark brown and sounds hollow when removed from the pan and tapped underneath. Transfer to a wire rack to cool.

Keep wrapped in waxed paper for at least 1 to 2 days before slicing thinly. This loaf will mature when kept and will taste best about 4 days after baking.

VARIATION

Raisin Pumpernickel

Put ½ cup raisins or golden raisins in a bowl, pour in enough orange juice to cover, and let soak for about 1 hour. Drain, then add the fruit to the dough just before shaping into a loaf. Proceed as in the main recipe.

Molasses produces the traditional dark color in this dense, rich bread made with a number of different flours, predominantly rye.

cheat's sourdough

Spelt flour has a nutty flavor and has recently become popular with organic farmers.

one-half 0.6 oz. cake compressed
yeast, crumbled*

2¾ cups water,
at room temperature

3⅓ cups spelt flour

1 tablespoon sea salt

about 2½ cups white bread flour,
plus extra for dusting

a large baking tray, floured

Makes 1 large loaf

**I have had variable results with
active dry yeast and prefer
compressed yeast for this recipe.*

Put the yeast in a bowl with half the water, and cream until smooth. Add 1¾ cups spelt flour and stir to make a thick batter. Cover with a damp cloth and set aside for 24 hours until it looks bubbly and slightly gray. Next day, stir in the remaining water to make a smooth batter. Transfer to a larger bowl, beat in the salt and remaining spelt flour with your hand, then gradually work in enough white flour to make a soft but not sticky dough (the amount depends on the quality of the spelt flour).

Turn out the dough onto a floured surface and knead for 10 minutes. If it sticks to your fingers, work in extra white flour, 1 tablespoon at a time. Return the dough to the bowl, cover with a damp cloth, and let rise at cool to normal room temperature until doubled in size—about 3 hours.

Uncover, punch down the dough, turn out onto a floured surface, and knead for 1 minute. It should be firm enough to hold its shape during baking; if too soft, work in extra flour, 1 tablespoon at a time.

Shape into a round loaf and place on the baking tray. Cover loosely and let rise as before until almost doubled in size—1½ to 2 hours. Uncover, then slash the top several times with a very sharp knife. Sprinkle with white flour, then bake in a preheated oven at 425°F for 20 minutes. Reduce the oven temperature to 400°F and bake for 15 minutes or until the loaf sounds hollow when tapped underneath. Remove from the oven and transfer to a wire rack to cool.

whole-wheat beer bread

2⅔ cups stone-ground
whole-wheat bread flour,
plus extra for dusting

⅔ cup coarsely ground
whole-wheat bread flour

2 teaspoons sea salt

0.6 oz. cake compressed yeast,
crumbled*

1 tablespoon lukewarm water

about 1½ cups beer,
at room temperature

a baking tray, greased

Makes 1 medium loaf

**To use active dry yeast, add
1 package to the flour, then
proceed with the recipe.
Omit the water and add
1 extra tablespoon of beer.*

Put the flours and salt in a large bowl and mix. Make a well in the center. Put the yeast and water in a small bowl and cream to a smooth paste.

Add the yeast paste and the beer to the well in the flour. Mix to a soft but not sticky dough, working it for several minutes before adding anything else.

The amount of liquid you need will depend on the flour, but the dough will feel very different from a white bread dough. If it seems very wet, add extra flour, 1 tablespoon at a time. If stiff and dry, with dry crumbs in the bottom of the bowl, work in extra beer or water, 1 tablespoon at a time.

Turn out the dough onto a floured surface and knead for 5 to 7 minutes until the dough is smooth and pliable. Return to the bowl, cover with a damp cloth, and let rise at normal room temperature until doubled in size—about 2 hours.

Punch down the risen dough and shape into a ball. Put on the baking tray, cover loosely with a damp cloth, and let rise again as before until doubled in size—about 1 hour.

Uncover the loaf, slash the top with a sharp knife, sprinkle with coarse whole-wheat flour, and bake in a preheated oven at 425°F for 30 to 35 minutes or until the loaf is golden brown and sounds hollow when tapped underneath. Remove from the oven and transfer to a wire rack to cool.

German-style smoked beer, brown ale, or stout give this bread strongest flavor: pale ale gives a more subtle taste.

FRUIT & NUTS

honeynut loaf

2½ cups stone-ground
whole-wheat bread flour

2½ cups unbleached
white bread flour,
plus extra for dusting

2½ teaspoons sea salt

0.6 oz. cake compressed yeast,
crumbled*

1½ cups water,
at room temperature

3 tablespoons flavorful honey

10 oz. nuts (any combination of
walnuts, hazelnuts, almonds,
cashews, or macadamias), lightly
toasted and coarsely chopped
(about 2½ cups)

2 baking sheets, greased

Makes 2 medium loaves

**To use active dry yeast, mix
1 package with the flour and salt,
add the water and honey, then
proceed with the recipe.*

Put the flours and salt in a large bowl, mix, then make a well in the center.

Put the yeast and a little of the water in a small bowl, and cream to a smooth liquid. Pour this mixture into the well in the flour.

Dissolve the honey in the rest of the water and add it to the well. Gradually work the flour into the liquid to make a soft but not sticky dough. If the dough sticks to your fingers, work in extra flour, about 1 tablespoon at a time. If there are dry crumbs in the bottom of the bowl, or the dough seems stiff and hard to work, add extra water, 1 tablespoon at a time.

Turn out the dough onto a lightly floured surface and knead thoroughly for 10 minutes until smooth and elastic.

Flatten the dough with your hand, sprinkle about one third of the nuts over the dough, then fold it over and over to distribute them evenly through the mixture.

Repeat this process twice, then shape the dough into a ball, and return it to the bowl.

Cover with a damp cloth and let rise at cool to normal room temperature until doubled in size—about 2 hours.

Uncover, punch down the risen dough with your knuckles, then turn out onto a floured surface and knead for 1 minute to ensure the nuts are evenly distributed.

Divide the dough in half. Shape each portion into a neat ball, pushing back any nuts that protrude or escape.

Put the balls of dough on a baking tray, cover as before, and let rise at cool to normal room temperature until doubled in size—about 1½ hours.

Uncover the risen loaves and slash the tops diagonally several times with a very sharp knife. Bake in a preheated oven at 425°F for about 15 minutes, then reduce the oven temperature to 375°F and bake for a further 20 to 25 minutes.

The loaves should sound hollow when removed from the baking tray and tapped underneath. Transfer to a wire rack to cool.

VARIATION

New England Maple Nut Loaf

A wonderful combination of traditional American ingredients; dried cranberries, maple syrup, and pecans.

Omit the roasted nuts from the main recipe and add ⅓ cup dried cranberries and 1½ cups pecans, broken into pieces. Substitute 3 tablespoons maple syrup instead of the honey, and proceed as in the main recipe.

Make this well-flavored bread with any combination of lightly toasted nuts, together with a strong-flavored honey, such as clover. Best served with butter, cream cheese, or cheese.

Use a good sugarless granola with ingredients such as raisins, dates, wheat flakes, oat flakes, apples, apricots, hazelnuts, almonds, and raisins.

granola round

Put the flours, muesli, and salt in a large bowl and mix well. Make a well in the center.

Put the yeast and 3 tablespoons of the milk mixture in a small bowl, and cream to a smooth liquid. Stir in the rest of the liquid, the honey, and oil, then pour into the well in the flour.

Gradually mix the dry ingredients into the liquid to make a fairly firm dough. If it seems dry or stiff, or there are dry crumbs in the bottom of the bowl, work in extra milk or water, 1 tablespoon at a time. If the dough sticks to your fingers, knead in extra white flour, 1 tablespoon at a time. The amount of liquid needed will depend on the muesli mix.

Turn out the dough onto a lightly floured surface and knead for about 5 minutes. Return the dough to the bowl, cover with a damp cloth, and leave at room temperature until doubled in size—1 to 1½ hours. Turn out onto a lightly floured surface and knead for 1 minute. Shape into a round loaf 8 inches across. Put on the prepared baking tray and score into 8 segments with a very sharp knife. Cover and let rise as before—for about 1 hour.

Uncover the loaf and sprinkle with whole-wheat flour. Cook in a preheated oven at 425°F for 30 minutes, or until it sounds hollow when tapped underneath. Remove from the oven and transfer to a wire rack to cool.

3⅓ cups white bread flour, plus extra for dusting

⅔ cup stone-ground whole-wheat flour

1⅔ cups unsweetened granola or muesli

2 teaspoons salt

0.6 oz. cake compressed yeast, crumbled*

about 1¾ cups equal mixture of milk and water, at room temperature

1 tablespoon honey

2 tablespoons vegetable oil

a baking tray, greased

Makes 1 large round loaf

*To use active dry yeast, mix 1 package with the flours, granola, and salt. Pour in all the liquids, then proceed with the recipe.

blue cheese and walnut twist

2 cups unbleached white bread flour, plus extra for dusting

1 teaspoon sea salt

¼ stick butter, chilled and diced

one-half 0.6 oz. cake compressed yeast, crumbled*

½ cup equal mixture of milk and water, at room temperature

1 egg, beaten

Blue Cheese and Walnut Filling

¾ cup cream cheese

1 tablespoon milk

½ cup finely ground walnuts

1 cup blue cheese

1 cup walnut pieces

freshly ground black pepper

a baking tray, greased

Makes 1 loaf

*To use active dry yeast, mix ½ package with the flour and salt, then proceed with the recipe.

Put the flour and salt in a large bowl and mix. Add the butter and rub it in with your fingertips until the mixture looks like fine crumbs. Make a well in the center.

Put the yeast and the milk and water mixture in a small bowl, and cream until smooth. Mix in the egg, then pour into the well in the flour. Gradually work in the flour to make a soft but not sticky dough.

Turn out onto a floured surface and knead for 10 minutes until smooth, silky, and elastic. Return the dough to the bowl, cover with a damp cloth, and let rise at normal room temperature until doubled in size—about 1 hour.

To make the filling, beat the cream cheese and milk until soft, then beat in the walnuts and pepper. In a separate bowl, crumble the blue cheese into small chunks, add the walnut pieces, and mix.

Uncover the risen dough and punch down, then roll out on a lightly floured surface into a rectangle, about 13 x 12 inches. Spread the cream cheese mixture over the top, then sprinkle with blue cheese and walnuts.

Roll up the dough fairly tightly from one long side, like a jelly roll, then roll this into a longer, thinner cylinder about 2 feet long. Cut in half lengthwise with a sharp knife. Twist the halves together, cut sides up, and shape into a neat ring on the baking tray.

Cover loosely with a damp cloth and let rise at room temperature until doubled in size—45 minutes to 1 hour.

Bake in a preheated oven at 400°F for 25 minutes, or until firm and golden. Remove from the oven and transfer to a wire rack to cool.

sour cherry loaf

A flavorful loaf, not too sweet—good with cold meat and pickles.

2⅓ cups unbleached white bread flour, plus extra for dusting

1 cup rye flour, stone-ground if possible

½ cup dried sour cherries

2 teaspoons sea salt

0.6 oz. cake compressed yeast, crumbled*

about 1¼ cups cold water

a baking tray, greased

Makes 1 medium loaf

*To use active dry yeast, add 1 package to the flour, then proceed with the recipe.

Put the flours, dried sour cherries, and salt in a large bowl, mix, then make a well in the center. Put the yeast and half the water in a small bowl and cream until smooth. Pour the yeast mixture into the well in the flour, add the remaining water, then gradually mix in the flour to make a soft but not sticky dough. If it seems sticky and difficult to work, mix in white flour, 1 tablespoon at a time. If stiff and dry, with crumbs in the bottom of the bowl, work in some water, 1 tablespoon at a time (the amount of liquid needed will depend on the quality of the flour).

Turn out the dough onto a lightly floured surface and knead for about 10 minutes until satiny and elastic. Return the dough to the bowl, cover with a damp cloth, and let rise at cool to normal room temperature until doubled in size—about 2 hours.

Uncover the dough, punch down, and turn out onto a lightly floured surface. Gently knead into an oval. With the edge of your hand, make a crease down the middle, then roll the dough over to make a sausage shape about 10 inches long. Place, seam side down, on the baking tray. Cover as before and let rise at normal room temperature until doubled in size—about 1 hour.

Uncover the loaf and slash several times across the top with a very sharp knife. Bake in a preheated oven at 425°F for 15 minutes until golden. Reduce the oven temperature to 375°F and bake for 10 to 15 minutes until the loaf sounds hollow when tapped underneath. Remove from the oven and transfer to a wire rack to cool.

VEGETABLES
& CHEESE

garlic knots

3⅓ cups white bread flour, plus extra for dusting

1½ teaspoons sea salt

one-half 0.6 oz. cake compressed yeast, crumbled*

1¼ cups cold water

1 tablespoon virgin olive oil

12 unpeeled garlic cloves

a pinch of salt

1 egg, beaten with a pinch of salt, to glaze

2 baking trays, greased

Makes 12

To use active dry yeast, mix ½ package with the flour and salt. Proceed with the recipe.

Roasted garlic produces a delicious aroma with no harsh taste.

Put the flour and salt in a large bowl and make a well in the center. Put the yeast and a little of the water in a small bowl and cream until smooth. Stir in the oil and the remaining water, then pour the yeast mixture into the well in the flour. Work in the flour to make a soft but not sticky dough. If too sticky, work in extra flour, 1 tablespoon at a time. If there are dry crumbs in the bowl, work in extra water, 1 tablespoon at a time.

Turn out the dough onto a floured surface and knead for 10 minutes until smooth, silky, and elastic. Return to the bowl, cover with a damp cloth, and let rise at cool to normal room temperature until doubled in size—1½ to 2 hours.

Put the garlic in a roasting pan and cook in a preheated oven at 375°F for 10 minutes until the skin is split and golden and the flesh soft and ripe-smelling. Let cool, then peel, sprinkle with salt, and mash into a coarse paste with the back of a knife.

Uncover the dough, punch down, then divide into 12 equal pieces. Shape each piece into a sausage about 8 inches long and flatten slightly. Spread the garlic paste on the top, then tie into knots. Place on the prepared baking trays, spacing them well apart, cover loosely with a damp cloth, and let rise until doubled in size—about 45 minutes. Brush with egg glaze, then bake in a preheated oven at 425°F for 10 to 15 minutes until the knots are golden brown and sound hollow when tapped underneath. Remove from the oven and transfer to a wire rack to cool.

onion rolls

Slow-cooked onion and rye flour give flavor without pungency.

Put the onion, sugar, and butter in a heavy saucepan and heat gently, stirring, until soft and slightly caramelized. Let cool.

Put the flours and salt in a bowl, mix, then make a well in the center. Put the yeast and a little water in a small bowl, and cream until smooth. Pour into the well in the flour and add the onion and remaining water. Work in the flour to make a soft but not sticky dough. If it sticks to your fingers or the bowl, work in extra white flour, 1 tablespoon at a time. If it seems stiff, with dry crumbs in the bowl, slowly work in extra water, 1 tablespoon at a time.

Turn out the dough onto a floured surface and knead for 10 minutes until very smooth and elastic. Return to the bowl, cover with a damp cloth, and let rise at cool to normal room temperature until doubled in size—1 to 1½ hours.

Uncover the dough and punch down. Turn out onto a floured surface and knead for 1 minute. Divide the dough into 14 equal pieces. Shape into balls and place well apart on the baking trays.

To make the onion shapes, pinch the centers, drawing them up to make a stalk. Cover with a damp cloth—to avoid flattening the stalks, use upturned bowls to support the cloth. Let rise for 30 minutes, until doubled in size.

Brush with egg glaze, then bake in a preheated oven at 425°F for about 15 to 20 minutes or until shiny golden brown. Remove from the oven and transfer to a wire rack to cool.

1 large onion, finely chopped

½ teaspoon sugar

2 tablespoons unsalted butter

2⅔ cups white bread flour, plus extra for dusting

⅔ cup rye flour, preferably stone-ground

2½ teaspoons sea salt

0.6 oz. cake compressed yeast, crumbled*

1¼ cups water, at room temperature

1 egg, beaten with a pinch of salt, to glaze

2 baking trays, greased

Makes 14

*To use active dry yeast, mix ½ package with the flours and salt, add the water and onion mixture, then proceed with the recipe.

Pumpkin makes a fine, soft, golden
bread that toasts well.

pumpkin bread

Peel the pumpkin or other squash and remove the seeds. Dice the flesh into
½-inch cubes—you will need 14 oz. in total.

Without adding water, cook the cubes in a steamer or microwave until they
soften. Put them in a food processor with the oil and process until smooth.
Let cool until just lukewarm, then mix in the salt and sugar.

Put the yeast and lukewarm water in a small bowl and cream to a smooth
paste. Mix the paste into the pumpkin purée.

Put the flour in a large bowl and make a well in the center. Spoon the purée
into the well, then mix in the flour to make a soft but not sticky dough. Turn
out onto a lightly floured surface and knead thoroughly for 5 minutes (or
3 minutes at low speed in a mixer with a dough hook).

Shape the dough into a round loaf about 7 inches across and put it on the
baking tray. Cover with a damp cloth and let rise at normal room temperature
until doubled in size—about 1½ hours.

Press your thumb into the middle of the risen loaf to make a small hollow,
then carefully brush the loaf with the egg glaze. Score the loaf into segments
with a sharp knife, then bake in a preheated oven at 400°F for about 30 minutes
or until it is golden brown and sounds hollow when tapped underneath.
Remove from the oven and transfer to a wire rack to cool.

**1 lb., 10 oz. pumpkin, Japanese
kabocha, or other winter squash**

1 tablespoon virgin olive oil

2½ teaspoons sea salt

2 teaspoons sugar

**0.6 oz. cake compressed yeast,
crumbled***

1 tablespoon lukewarm water

**2½ cups white bread flour,
plus extra for dusting**

**1 egg, beaten with a pinch
of salt, to glaze**

a baking tray, greased

Makes 1 medium loaf

**To use active dry yeast, mix
1 package with the flour, then work
in the pumpkin purée. If the dough
seems dry or there are dry crumbs
in the bottom of the bowl, work in
a little cold water.*

easy cheesy brioche

A rich, light, tangy loaf—and easily made in a mixer, unlike a classic brioche. Serve it with cheese, salad, or soup.

Put the yeast in the bowl of a free-standing mixer. Pour in the milk and mix using the beater attachment. Beat in the eggs, followed by the salt and cayenne pepper.

Using the dough hook at low speed, gradually work in the flour to make a soft but not sticky dough. Knead in the machine at low speed for another 5 minutes until smooth and elastic.

Add the softened butter and knead for another 3 to 4 minutes until completely mixed. Cover with a damp towel and let rise at normal room temperature until doubled in size—about 1½ hours.

Knead the grated cheese into the dough for about 1 minute at low speed, then turn out onto a floured surface and shape into a loaf to fit the pan.

Put the dough in the pan, then cover with a damp cloth and leave at normal room temperature until doubled in size—about 1 hour (the dough should just reach the rim of the pan).

Gently brush the risen loaf with egg glaze, taking care not to glue it to the sides of the pan.

Sprinkle with the extra cheese and bake in a preheated oven at 400°F for about 35 minutes or until it turns golden brown and sounds hollow when turned out of the pan and tapped underneath. Remove from the oven, turn out of the pan, and transfer the loaf to a wire rack to cool.

0.6 oz. cake compressed yeast, crumbled*

½ cup lukewarm skim milk

2 eggs

1 teaspoon sea salt

¼ teaspoon cayenne pepper

2 cups white bread flour, plus extra for dusting

½ stick unsalted butter, softened

1 cup Gruyère cheese, grated, plus ¼ cup extra, to finish

1 egg, beaten with a large pinch of salt, to glaze

a loaf pan, 1 lb., greased

Makes 1 medium loaf

*To use active dry yeast, mix 1 package with the flour and work into the liquids in the bowl. Proceed with the recipe.

cheese rolls with cheddar and onion

4⅓ cups unbleached white bread flour, plus extra for dusting

2 teaspoons sea salt

1 teaspoon mustard powder

2 cups grated sharp Cheddar cheese

⅓ cup finely chopped scallions

0.6 oz. cake compressed yeast, crumbled*

1 cup skim milk, at room temperature

¾ cup water, at room temperature

vegetable oil, for greasing bowl

milk, for glazing

2 baking trays, lightly greased

Makes 12

To use active dry yeast, add 1 package to the flour, then proceed with the recipe.

Put the flour, salt, mustard powder, 1½ cups of the cheese, and the scallions in a large bowl and mix. Make a well in the center.

Put the yeast and the milk in a small bowl, and cream to a smooth liquid. Stir in the water, then pour into the well in the flour. Gradually work the flour into the liquid to make a soft but not sticky dough.

Turn out the dough onto a floured surface and knead for 10 minutes until it feels smooth and elastic. It can also be kneaded for 5 minutes at low speed in a mixer fitted with a dough hook. Put the dough into a lightly oiled bowl, turning the dough so the entire surface is lightly coated with oil. Cover with a damp cloth and let rise until doubled in size—1½ to 2 hours.

Uncover the dough, punch down, then turn out onto a floured surface and knead for a few seconds. Divide the dough into 12 equal parts and pat into ovals about 4½ x 3 x 1 inch. Arrange well apart on the baking trays. Brush with milk, then sprinkle with the remaining cheese. Let rise until doubled in size—about 30 minutes.

Press your thumb into the middle of each roll, then bake in a preheated oven at 425°F for 15 minutes or until golden. Remove from the oven and transfer to a wire rack to cool.

For the best flavor, use sharp cheese: much so-called Cheddar is too bland for this recipe.

index

CONVERSION CHARTS

Weights and measures have been rounded up or down slightly to make measuring easier.

VOLUME EQUIVALENTS:

AMERICAN	METRIC	IMPERIAL
1 teaspoon	5 ml	
1 tablespoon	15 ml	
¼ cup	60 ml	2 fl.oz.
⅓ cup	75 ml	2½ fl.oz.
½ cup	125 ml	4 fl.oz.
⅔ cup	150 ml	5 fl.oz. (¼ pint)
¾ cup	175 ml	6 fl.oz.
1 cup	250 ml	8 fl.oz.

WEIGHT EQUIVALENTS: MEASUREMENTS:

IMPERIAL	METRIC	INCHES	CM
1 oz.	25 g	¼ inch	5 mm
2 oz.	50 g	½ inch	1 cm
3 oz.	75 g	¾ inch	1.5 cm
4 oz.	125 g	1 inch	2.5 cm
5 oz.	150 g	2 inches	5 cm
6 oz.	175 g	3 inches	7 cm
7 oz.	200 g	4 inches	10 cm
8 oz. (½ lb.)	250 g	5 inches	12 cm
9 oz.	275 g	6 inches	15 cm
10 oz.	300 g	7 inches	18 cm
11 oz.	325 g	8 inches	20 cm
12 oz.	375 g	9 inches	23 cm
13 oz.	400 g	10 inches	25 cm
14 oz.	425 g	11 inches	28 cm
15 oz.	475 g	12 inches	30 cm
16 oz. (1 lb.)	500 g		
2 1b.	1 kg		

OVEN TEMPERATURES:

110˚C	(225˚F)	Gas ¼
120˚C	(250˚F)	Gas ½
140˚C	(275˚F)	Gas 1
150˚C	(300˚F)	Gas 2
160˚C	(325˚F)	Gas 3
180˚C	(350˚F)	Gas 4
190˚C	(375˚F)	Gas 5
200˚C	(400˚F)	Gas 6
220˚C	(425˚F)	Gas 7
230˚C	(450˚F)	Gas 8
240˚C	(475˚F)	Gas 9

credits

All photographs by **Patrice de Villiers** unless otherwise stated.

Martin Brigdale Endpapers, pages 1 above left, 2, 4, 7 center left & center right, 8–9, 10, 13, 27, 29 left, 35, 39 center, 43, 49 center and right, 59, 62, 67–70, 72, 73, 83, 89, 101 center, 107, 113 left & center, 129 center, 139 left & center, 144, 180–1, 182, 185 center, 196, 119, 203, 209, 215, 217 center, 227 left, 240

Peter Cassidy Pages 1 above right, 7 right, 101 right, 113 right, 159 center & right, 185 left & right, 197, 227 center

Debi Treloar Pages 5, 29 center & right, 39 left & right, 49 left, 126, 145 right

Nicky Dowey Pages 7 left, 171 right, 217 right

Vanessa Davies Pages 129 right, 171 center

Jean Cazals Page 145 left

Christine Hanscomb Page 6

Jeremy Hopley Page 217 left

William Lingwood Pages 124–5

David Munns Page 227 right

Craig Robertson Page 159 left

Ian Wallace Page 101 left